A Soft Pillow for an Armadillo

Donna Alvermann
Connie A. Bridge
Barbara A. Schmidt
Lyndon W. Searfoss
Peter Winograd
Scott G. Paris

D.C. Heath and Company
HEATH Lexington, Massachusetts Toronto, Ontario

Acknowledgments

Grateful acknowledgment is made for permission to reprint the following copyrighted material.

Asimov, Isaac. **The Best New Thing,** copyright © 1971 by Isaac Asimov. Reprinted by permission of the Author.

Barrett, Judi. **Animals Should Definitely Not Wear Clothing.** Text copyright © 1970 by Judi Barrett. Drawings copyright © 1970 by Ron Barrett. Reprinted by permission of Macmillan Publishing Company.

Byars, Betsy. **Me and Goat McGee;** copyright © 1984 by Betsy Byars; reprinted by permission of the Author.

Cameron, Ann. **"Gloria Who Might Be My Best Friend,"** from *The Stories Julian Tells;* copyright © 1981 by Ann Cameron. Reprinted by permission of Random House, Inc.

Cameron, Eleanor. **"Greg's Bike,"** adapted from *That Julia Redfern,* by Eleanor Cameron. Text copyright © 1982 by Eleanor Cameron. Reprinted by permission of the publisher, E. P. Dutton, a division of NAL Penguin, Inc.

Carrick, Carol. **Patrick's Dinosaurs,** by Carol and Donald Carrick. Text copyright © 1983 by Carol Carrick. Reprinted by permission of Clarion Books/Ticknor & Fields, a Houghton Mifflin Company. **Whatever Happened to Patrick's Dinosaurs?** by Carol and Donald Carrick. Text copyright © 1986 by Carol Carrick. Reprinted by permission of Clarion Books/Ticknor & Fields, a Houghton Mifflin Company.

Charlip, Remy, and Burton Supree. **Harlequin and the Gift of Many Colors,** copyright © 1973 by Remy Charlip and Burton Supree. Adapted by permission of the authors.

Cole, William. **"Back Yard, July Night"** is reprinted by permission of the Author.

Coutant, Helen. **The Gift,** copyright © 1983 by Helen Coutant. Adapted by permission Alfred A. Knopf, Inc.

de Rodríguez, Neli Garrido. **"The Armadillo,"** from *Legendas Argentinas,* copyright © 1981 by Neli Garrido de Rodríguez. Reprinted by permission (Editorial Plus Ultra).

Fenton, Edward. **Probably,** copyright © 1984 by Edward Fenton. Reprinted by permission of the Author.

Flora, James. The abridged version of **My Friend Charlie,** copyright © 1964 by James Flora, is reprinted by permission of Harcourt Brace Jovanovich, Inc.

Hadithi, Mwenye. **Greedy Zebra;** copyright © 1984 by Mwenye Hadithi; reprinted by permission of Little, Brown and Company and Hodder and Stoughton Children's Books.

Low, Alice. **Herbert's Treasure,** copyright © 1971 by Alice Low. Reprinted by permission of the Author.

McMillan, Bruce, and Brett McMillan. From **Puniddles.** Copyright © 1982 by Bruce McMillan. Reprinted by permission of Houghton Mifflin Company.

Mooser, Stephen. **"A Very Strange Photo,"** from *Images.* Copyright © 1977 by Stephen Mooser. Reprinted by permission of Curtis Brown Ltd.

Noble, Trinka Hakes. **The Day Jimmy's Boa Ate the Wash.** Text copyright © 1980 by Trinka Hakes Noble. Reprinted by permission of Dial Books for Young Readers.

Pedersen, Ruth Dana. **The First True Bicycle.** Copyright © 1973 by Ruth Dana Pedersen. Reprinted by permission of *Highlights for Children,* Columbus, Ohio.

Prelutsky, Jack. **"Michael Built a Bicycle,"** from *The New Kid on the Block,* by Jack Prelutsky. Copyright © 1984 by Jack Prelutsky. Reprinted by permission of Greenwillow Books (a division of William Morrow & Co.).

Schmidt, Barbara A. **"Hey, Smarty . . . Zoo Party,"** from *Finnigan and Friends.* Copyright © 1987 by Curriculum Associates, Inc. Reprinted by permission.

Silverstein, Shel. **"Hot Dog,"** from *A Light in the Attic,* by Shel Silverstein. Copyright © 1981 by Snake Eye Music, Inc. Reprinted by permission of Harper & Row, Publishers, Inc.

Strauss, Linda L. **No Dogs Is Not Enough.** Copyright © 1984 by Linda Leopold Strauss. Reprinted by permission of the Author.

Teal, William. **"Blast Off!"** from *3, 2, 1, Contact* magazine. Copyright © 1987 by Children's Television Workshop. Used by permission of Children's Television Workshop.

(Continued on page 336)

Published simultaneously in Canada

Printed in the United States of America

International Standard Book Number: 0-669-23532-6

3 4 5 6 7 8 9 0

Table of Contents

1

A Pet? You Bet!

Imagine That!

2

Click!

What Will I Wear?

3

Spokes and Sprockets

Hidden Treasures

A Soft Pillow for an Armadillo

If you had all these pets—two zebras, four chimpanzees, one armadillo, half a dozen frogs, a lion cub, and three peacocks—how many tails would your pets have altogether?

7 (Chimpanzees and frogs don't have tails.)

A Pet? You Bet!

HEY, SMARTY...
ZOO PARTY!

Hey, smarty! Hey, smarty! I'm having a party.
Please come, but you must bring a pet.
Make it a weird one,
A strange but not feared one
That's never been seen by a vet.

I've got a soft pillow for an armadillo
Chimpanzees are good for a laugh.
A hippo that's happy
A croc that is snappy
Or even baby giraffe.

Hey, smarty! Hey, smarty! I'm having a party.
Please come, but you must bring a pet.
Make it a weird one,
A strange but not feared one
That's never been seen by a vet.

10

How about an iguana or even a llama?
There's room for a camel out back.
A bear that is cuddly
A pig not too muddly
Or even a three-legged yak.

Hey, smarty! Hey, smarty! I'm having a party.
Please come, but you must bring a pet.
Make it a weird one,
A strange but not feared one
That's never been seen by a vet.

So bring your anteater (A penguin is neater),
A walrus will add to the fun.
There's a problem or two
When my folks see our zoo
You'd better be ready to run!

—*Barbara Schmidt*

11

No Dogs Is Not Enough

by Linda Leopold Strauss

Tina wanted a dog.

Tina's mother said no.

Mrs. Lawlor who lived up the street promised Tina one of Snuffy's puppies—if Tina's mother said yes.

Tina's mother said no.

"I have enough to do already," she told Tina, "without taking care of a dog."

The Lawlors were going to put an ad in the paper to sell Snuffy's puppies, even the brown puppy with the white nose. Tina had to find a way to change her mother's mind.

The next morning, after she got dressed, Tina found a rope. She made a loop at one end and a smaller loop at the other end that she held in her hand. Then she ran downstairs, trailing the rope behind her.

"I'm going to walk Nosey before breakfast," Tina told her mother.

Her mother stared at her.

"Nosey is my dog," said Tina. "Isn't she cute?" Then Tina went out the back door, pulling the rope behind her.

"Now, Tina . . . ," began her mother, but Tina was gone.

When she came back into the kitchen, she
looped the rope over the back of her chair.
"Down, Nosey," she said. "Down, girl. Sit."

Tina's father leaned over to look at the floor
next to Tina's chair. He looked at Tina. "Are you
feeling all right?" he asked.

"Fine," said Tina. "Nosey's fine, too. She's a
good dog, isn't she, Dad?"

"You'd never even know she's there," said
Tina's father.

Tina was very busy after school. She took the
money she had been saving from her allowance
and walked Nosey to the corner store. She
bought dog food and a red dish to put it in, a
leash, and a real leather collar. When she got
home, she put the dog food and a bowl of water
in the kitchen.

"Mom?" said Tina. "Nosey's such a good dog. Can she sleep in my room tonight?"

"Absolutely not," said Tina's mother firmly. "No dogs in the bedroom." Then she laughed out loud. "You and your imagination!"

After a few days, the neighbors got used to seeing Tina walk around the block with a leash and a real leather dog collar. Tina walked Nosey twice a day, rain or shine, and every morning she put fresh food in her new red bowl. Tina's mother had to admit that Tina took good care of Nosey.

"If I can take care of Nosey," Tina told her mother, "I can take care of any puppy."

"Perhaps," said her mother, "but we have Nosey now. One dog is enough."

Early the next morning, Tina came down to the kitchen. "Have you seen Nosey?" she asked her mother. "I can't find her anywhere."

She walked over to the red dish. "Nosey hasn't touched her food," she said in a worried voice. "She must have got out."

"But how?" asked Tina's mother. "You had her with you at bedtime. I saw her myself." She turned to Tina's father. "Didn't you, dear?" she asked.

Tina's father looked at her and shook his head. "You and your imagination!" he laughed. "You and that dog!"

Right after breakfast, Tina went out to search for Nosey. She walked up driveways and behind houses and down the hill to the playground.

"Nosey," she called, but Nosey didn't come.

"Maybe we should put an ad in the paper," suggested Tina's mother at lunchtime.

"What would we say Nosey looked like?" Tina wanted to know.

There was no doubt about it. Nosey was going to be hard to find.

"We won't find her," said Tina, and she was right.

"I hate to admit it," said Tina's mother at dinner, "but I think I miss Nosey."

"We could get another dog," said Tina quickly.

"What if Nosey comes back?" asked her father. "Your mother says one dog is enough."

"Nosey is not coming back," said Tina. "And no dogs is not enough."

"Not coming back?" said her mother. "That's a different story." She looked at Tina. "I see in the paper that Lawlors' puppies are still for sale."

"Brown ones," said Tina's father. "One with a white nose."

Tina held her breath.

"It's a nice night," said Tina's father. "Let's take a walk to the Lawlors'."

"And don't forget the leash and collar," said Tina's mother.

HOT DOG

from A LIGHT IN THE ATTIC

I have a hot dog for a pet,
The only kind my folks would let
Me get.
He does smell sort of bad
And yet,
He absolutely never gets
The sofa wet.
We have a butcher for a vet,
The strangest vet you ever met.
Guess we're the weirdest family yet,
To have a hot dog for a pet.

—*Shel Silverstein*

Think About It

1. What do the last two lines of "Hey, Smarty . . . Zoo Party!" mean?
2. Why did Tina's mother say no when Tina asked for a puppy?
3. What was Tina's plan for getting a dog? Did her plan work?
4. What did Tina mean by "No dogs is not enough"?
5. How is the poem "Hot Dog" like "No Dogs Is Not Enough"?

Create and Share
Make a list of four things you could do with an imaginary pet. Find a partner. Act out the things on your list and see if your partner can guess your pet.

Explore
Find another poem by Shel Silverstein to read or any other poem about a pet.

The Day Jimmy's Boa Ate the Wash

by Trinka Hakes Noble

"How was your class trip to the farm?"

"Oh . . . boring . . . kind of dull . . . until the cow started crying."

"A cow . . . crying?"

"Yeah, you see, a haystack fell on her."

"But a haystack doesn't just fall over."

"It does if a farmer crashes into it with his tractor."

"Oh, come on, a farmer wouldn't do that."

"He would if he were too busy yelling at the pigs to get off our school bus."

"What were the pigs doing on the bus?"

"Eating our lunches."

"Why were they eating your lunches?"

"Because we threw their corn at each other, and they didn't have anything else to eat."

"Well, that makes sense, but why were you throwing corn?"

"Because we ran out of eggs."

"Out of eggs? Why were you throwing eggs?"

"Because of the boa constrictor."

"*The Boa Constrictor!*"

"Yeah, Jimmy's pet boa constrictor."

"What was Jimmy's pet boa constrictor doing on the farm?"

"Oh, he brought it to meet all the farm animals, but the chickens didn't like it."

"You mean he took it into the hen house?"

"Yeah, and the chickens started squawking and flying around."

"Go on, go on. What happened?"

"Well, one hen got excited and laid an egg, and it landed on Jenny's head."

"The hen?"

"No, the egg. And it broke—yucky—all over her hair."

"What did she do?"

"She got mad because she thought Tommy threw it, so she threw one at him."

"What did Tommy do?"

"Oh, he ducked and the egg hit Marianne in the face. So she threw one at Jenny but she missed and hit Jimmy, who dropped his boa constrictor."

"Oh, and I know, the next thing you knew, everyone was throwing eggs, right?"

"Right."

"And when you ran out of eggs, you threw the pigs' corn, right?"

"Right again."

"Well, what finally stopped it?"

"Well, we heard the farmer's wife screaming."

"Why was she screaming?"

"We never found out, because Mrs. Stanley made us get on the bus, and we sort of left in a hurry without the boa constrictor."

"I bet Jimmy was sad because he left his pet boa constrictor."

"Oh, not really.   We left in such a hurry that one of the pigs didn't get off the bus, so now he's got a pet pig."

"Boy, that sure sounds like an exciting trip."

"Yeah, I suppose, if you're the kind of kid who likes class trips to the farm."

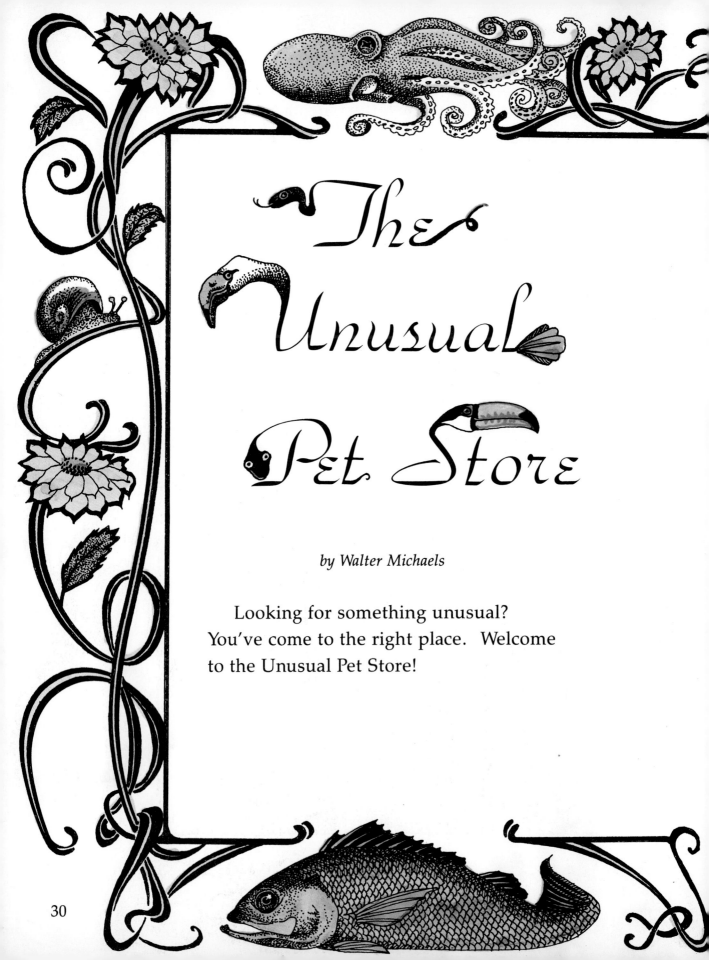

The Unusual Pet Store

by Walter Michaels

Looking for something unusual?
You've come to the right place. Welcome
to the Unusual Pet Store!

You won't find any dogs or cats in this pet store. There are no parakeets, no goldfish, and no hamsters here either. In fact, this pet store doesn't have any of the animals people *usually* think of when they think of pets.

However, it does have pet crickets! Just come over here to the insect corner. There's one chirping away in a big jar. That means it's a male. They're the ones that sing.

Crickets have been favorite pets in China for thousands of years. Besides making music, they are said to bring good luck. Never keep two crickets together in the same jar or they will fight. Put sand and leafy twigs in the bottom of the jar and be sure your pet cricket has water. A soaked piece of cotton will do the trick. As for food, crickets will eat bits of almost anything from your refrigerator.

Listen to that peaceful chirping. With a cricket as a pet, you'll feel as if you're on a camp-out in your own bedroom.

How about a pet bird? I mean
something a little more unusual than a
parakeet. Look out the back window.
Do you see that bird with the beautiful
tail? That's a peacock! Imagine having a
peacock for a pet. It wouldn't be easy.
Peacocks cost a lot more money than
parakeets, and they need plenty of room
outside to walk around. Not only are
they beautiful, but they make very good
watchdogs. Have you ever heard a
peacock's cry? It could wake up the
whole neighborhood.

Maybe you'd rather have a nice quiet boa constrictor. This one in the giant cage is called Cuddles. She's asleep right now. She just had lunch. She's about ten feet long and very gentle, as long as she has enough room. That's why her glass cage is so big. You'll notice it has a swimming pool. Boas love to take a dip! The thick branches are for climbing. There's also a brick on the bottom of the cage. Cuddles rubs up against this to help her wriggle out of her old, itchy snakeskin.

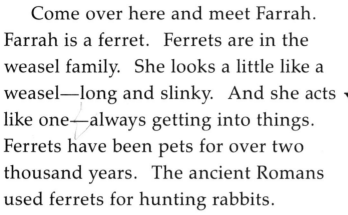

Come over here and meet Farrah. Farrah is a ferret. Ferrets are in the weasel family. She looks a little like a weasel—long and slinky. And she acts like one—always getting into things. Ferrets have been pets for over two thousand years. The ancient Romans used ferrets for hunting rabbits.

You can feed ferrets dog food or cat food. They're very friendly. They are smarter than cats, and you can train them almost as easily as dogs. You can even walk them like dogs, on a leash. I have a big outdoor cage for Farrah, with a warm nest for sleeping.

Taking care of any animal is a big job, whether the animal is a cricket or a cat. It means keeping your pet clean and healthy, and making sure it has enough food and exercise.

If you plan to take care of a pet, especially an unusual one, you'd better find out as much as you can about that animal and what it needs. Many animals should not be pets. A baby bobcat may be cute and tame when it's tiny, but when it grows up—watch out!

Here in the Unusual Pet Store, you don't have to worry. There are no impossible pets here—just the usual unusual ones.

Think About It

1. What started all the excitement at the farm?
2. Why was the farmer's wife screaming?
3. Do you think the farmer and his wife will invite the class to the farm again? Why or why not?
4. Why do you think many animals do not make good pets?

Create and Share

Imagine what might happen if Jimmy brought his boa constrictor to school!   Describe a chain of problems that might occur.

Explore

Read about more adventures with Jimmy and his boa or find a book about a pet that causes trouble. Share what happens with a friend.

Chuka's Hawk

by Elizabeth B. Whitmore

Chuka was standing on the roof of his father's house, keeping well away from the corner where Big Brother kept his pet. As Chuka looked at the pet eagle, he saw the sun. Only a small bit of it showed above the mountains. Big Brother would come home soon to feed the eagle.

Chuka stopped playing and watched the road. Soon he saw Big Brother coming, his bow and arrow in his hand and his hunting bag full.

Big Brother climbed onto the roof. The eagle tugged at its chain and cried out loudly. Big Brother tossed food to his eagle, and the eagle ate it quickly.

Chuka looked at the eagle with longing. "I want a pet eagle, too," he said.

"No, you are too little," said Big Brother.

Mother called them to dinner. When they were done, Chuka helped his mother clear away the dishes and wash them.

In the morning, Chuka went out to play with Grandfather's new puppy, Bakito. When Big Brother came along, Chuka called, "Take me with you to herd the sheep, Big Brother."

"You are too little," said Big Brother, laughing.

Chuka watched Big Brother start down the road. Then he went to see his uncle. "You do not look happy, Chuka," his uncle said.

"I want a pet eagle," said Chuka. "Will you help me catch one?"

"An eagle cannot be a pet," said his uncle. "Your brother's eagle will never make a good pet. But you can make a hawk a pet if you try very hard. Tomorrow I will help you hunt for a hawk."

The next morning, Chuka and his uncle walked and walked. Soon, Chuka heard bird sounds from high in the air. He looked up. "Those are hawks," said his uncle. "We are in a good place. Look for a hawk in a tree."

Chuka's uncle walked ahead, looking and looking. Chuka saw a young hawk on a low branch of a tree. He watched it swoop to the ground, snap up a bug, and then fly back to the branch again.

Chuka caught some bugs. He held them in his hands while he took off his shirt. Then he threw the bugs on the ground in front of the hawk. When the hawk swooped down to snap them up, Chuka threw his shirt over the bird and caught it. The hawk tried to get away, but Chuka held on.

When Chuka's uncle came back, he asked, "What do you have there, Chuka?"

"A young hawk!" cried Chuka.

"You caught a hawk?" His uncle was surprised.

They carried the hawk home. Chuka tied it by a rope on the top of the house, as far away from Big Brother's eagle as he could. The hawk snapped its bill at the eagle.

"My hawk is not afraid of the eagle!" cried Chuka.

"Remember, you can make it a pet," said his uncle.

Every day Chuka went hunting. When he could find a mouse, he gave it to his hawk. When he couldn't, he caught bugs. One day he petted the hawk's head. It did not snap at him. After that, Chuka petted the hawk's head whenever he gave it food.

The hawk liked Chuka. It rubbed its bill on Chuka's cheek and perched on his shoulder. One day, Chuka took his hawk for a walk. The hawk sat on Chuka's shoulder. It was becoming a pet. Chuka named his pet Wiki.

It was now time for Big Brother to learn how to weave. Grandfather would teach him. Father would need help herding the sheep.

"Come with me, Chuka," said Father. "It is time for you to learn to herd."

After many weeks, Father said, "Bring the young dog, Bakito, today. He, too, must learn to work." As soon as Bakito had learned to herd, Father said, "I am needed in the fields to plant the corn and beans. You are big enough to herd the sheep, Chuka. Bakito will help you watch them."

Chuka felt very big and brave as he set out with only Bakito. But when he was out in the desert, he did not feel big. He did not feel brave. The desert was hot and quiet and as empty as the sky. The day was as long as a week.

That night Chuka said to his father, "May I take Wiki with me when I go into the desert tomorrow?"

"Will you play with the hawk and forget to watch the sheep?" asked Father.

"Oh, no," said Chuka.

"Then you may take Wiki," said Father.

"Your hawk will fly away," said Big Brother.

The next morning when Chuka left to herd the sheep, Wiki was perched on his shoulder. Every day Chuka herded the sheep with Wiki and Bakito to help.

Bakito chased rabbits. Wiki found some grasshoppers and snapped them up. Sometimes his sharp eyes saw a mouse, and he swooped down on it. Once he left Chuka's shoulder and flew up, up until he was flying with some other hawks.

Chuka watched the hawks until he could not tell which one was Wiki. He was afraid Wiki would not come back. But soon a hawk began to fly down in big circles. As it got closer to the ground, the circles got smaller and smaller. Then, when it was quite low, it swooped down and bit Bakito on the ear. Bakito howled loudly, but Chuka was so glad Wiki had come back that he laughed and laughed.

One day Bakito was chasing rabbits, and high in the air Wiki was playing with the other hawks. Suddenly an animal began chasing the sheep. It looked like a dog, but Chuka knew it was a hungry coyote! The coyote wanted a lamb to eat—one of his father's lambs.

Chuka found a big stick. He waved the stick at the coyote and shouted, but the coyote did not run away.

"Bakito! Wiki! Help! Help!" cried Chuka.

The hawk heard Chuka. Wiki did not sail
down in big circles this time. He folded his
wings and swooped down from the sky like an
arrow. He put his claws into the coyote's back.
The coyote ran away, howling with pain. Then
Wiki flew to Chuka and perched on his shoulder.
He rubbed Chuka's cheek with his bill.

47

That evening when the dishes were cleared
away, Chuka said, "Tonight I have a story to tell."
Then he told about the coyote. He told about the
big stick. He told about Wiki and Bakito.

When the story was finished, Father said, "My
son, you have done well. Tomorrow you may
choose a lamb to have for your very own."

Big Brother went into the storeroom. He came
back with his best arrow in his hand. He gave it
to Chuka. "I will help you make a bigger bow,"
he said.

Chuka was very proud. It was good to have a
lamb and to be able to have a pet hawk. But,
most of all, it was good to be able to go in the
desert—and not be afraid.

Think About It

1. What did Chuka do to help the hawk become his pet?
2. Why did Chuka and Wiki need one another?
3. How did Wiki help Chuka grow up?
4. Which of the pets you've read about in A PET? YOU BET! is the most unusual? Explain.

Create and Share   Imagine a time when Wiki is in trouble and Chuka comes to the rescue. Tell what happens in a paragraph that describes the adventure.

Explore   Find out more about hawks by looking in the encyclopedia.

Imagine That !

In what nation can a kite be a bird?

Why, the imagine nation, of course!

PROBABLY

by Edward Fenton

Simon and Maria lived in the same town and on the same block and always walked to school together. They were in the same classroom, and when school was over they walked home together.

One day they saw a fire truck blocking the street. There was a cat high up in a tree, and the firefighters were trying to get it down.

"I wonder," said Simon, "how that cat got up so high?"

"I think," said Maria, "that there must be a circus in town."

"A circus? What would a circus have to do with the cat up in the tree?" Simon wanted to know.

"Well," said Maria, "the circus must've had a parade, and the cat was right in the middle of the street. Probably an elephant picked that cat up with his trunk and put it up there so he wouldn't step on it."

"Oh," said Simon. "I never thought of that!"

The next morning, when they were walking to school, they saw a gray-haired woman wearing a red raincoat and tennis shoes. She had dropped a letter in the mailbox and was carefully making sure that it didn't stick in the slot.

"I wonder," said Simon, "who she has written to? That must be a very important letter."

"I think," said Maria, "that she has a son who is an explorer. Right now he's on a dangerous expedition in the middle of the desert, but he ran out of food and water and everything. Probably," she said, "his mother is sending him money, so that he can buy more food and stuff and go on with his expedition."

"Oh," said Simon. "I never thought of that!"

On Thursday, they stopped at the red traffic light. Just then they saw a long automobile streak through it.

"I wonder why that driver didn't wait for the light to change?" said Simon.

"Probably that's a getaway car from the biggest bank robbery of all time," said Maria.

"Why aren't the police chasing it?" asked Simon.

"Because they haven't caught on yet," said Maria.

"Why would the robbers go right through a red light? You'd think they'd be afraid of getting arrested and then getting caught with the loot."

"Don't be simple, Simon," said Maria. "That is just the second getaway car. The rest of the robbers are going in the other direction. Probably," she said, "driving through a red light was only to direct the police away from the real getaway car."

"Oh," said Simon. "I never thought of that!"

The next day when they were walking to school, they saw a truck with a long trailer carrying a huge tree.

"What's that big tree doing on that truck?" said Simon.

"They must be taking that tree to a sailor," said Maria.

"Why would a sailor want a tree like that?" demanded Simon.

"He must have been shipwrecked on an island in the middle of the Pacific Ocean," said Maria. "And, by the time he was rescued, the natives had become fond of him, so they gave him a lot of farewell presents."

"Like what?" asked Simon.

"Monkeys and parrots. That's all they had to give him. But when he got home, he couldn't have all those animals in the house. Probably," Maria said, "that sailor is going to plant the tree in his garden so that all those monkeys and parrots can swing in it as much as they like."

"Oh," said Simon. "I never thought of that!"

The next day when Maria called for him, Simon was not ready for school.

"Hurry up, Simon," said Maria. "We'll be late."

Simon did not say anything. He just got his books, and they set off.

When they reached the schoolyard, it was empty. The building was locked.

"What's happened?" asked Maria. "Where is everybody?"

"Probably," said Simon with a grin, "everybody is home. It's a holiday today."

"Oh," said Maria. "I never thought of that!"

Think About It

1. Why did the author title this story "Probably"?
2. Do you think Simon liked to ask Maria questions on purpose? Why or why not?
3. Tell why you think Maria's stories could or could not really have happened.
4. What did you think about Simon's answer at the end of the story?

Create and Share   Choose one of Simon's questions from the story that begins, "I wonder . . . " Now make up an unusual or funny explanation, as Maria did. Start with, "Probably . . . "

Explore   Ask members in your family the most imaginative children's story they remember. With your classmates, make a chart of the answers you get.

The Imagination of Walt Disney

by H. Barclay Holmes

One Friday afternoon, just before the bell, George's teacher told the class to quiet down. "I have some homework for all of you," he said.

The whole class groaned. Especially George.

"This weekend," the teacher said, "I want you to write a story about a trip to a place you have never been. Write about a place you would like to see. Use your imagination!"

George couldn't believe it! He wanted to play baseball all weekend, not write any silly stories! How was he going to write a story about a place he had never been?

The teacher told them to go to the library if they needed ideas for their stories. So on Saturday morning George went to the library and walked along the tall stacks of books.

"Which book do I look at first?" he wondered. There seemed to be so many books! George leaned back on one of the bookshelves. Books, and books, and more books! All of a sudden, a big, white book fell off the shelf and bumped him on the head! "What? Who did that?" he cried.

But no one was there.

George picked up the book and looked at it. It was thick and dusty. Inside there were pictures of Donald Duck, Snow White and the Seven Dwarfs, and Mary Poppins. The book was about a man named Walt Disney. It said he was the "imagination" behind all these characters.

"If I had an imagination, I could do my homework in no time," George said.

George sat down on the carpet and began to read more about Walt Disney and his imagination. The book said that Walt Disney was born in Chicago on December 5, 1901. Then his family moved to Missouri, where Walt became friends with another boy named Walt. "The Two Walts" liked to dress up as President Lincoln and Charlie Chaplin and put on skits for their classmates. This was one of the first ways Disney used his imagination to entertain people.

When Disney grew up, he realized that he really liked to draw pictures and cartoons. So he started making his own Laugh-o-Grams. Laugh-o-Grams were short cartoons that came between longer movies.

On a train ride across the country, Disney had an idea for a different cartoon. He told his wife Lillian about it. It was about a funny, little mouse named Mortimer who could talk, whistle, and sing.

"That sounds like a good idea," his wife said. "But don't call him Mortimer."

So Disney called him Mickey.

In 1928 Mickey Mouse was in the first sound cartoon called *Steamboat Willie*. Suddenly Walt Disney and Mickey Mouse were famous stars!

"That's what I need. A good idea!" George said.

George read on.

Walt Disney, with the help of his friends, made more movies. Some of these were *Snow White and the Seven Dwarfs*, *Pinocchio*, *Swiss Family Robinson*, and *Mary Poppins*, to name a few.

Later Disney hosted a television show, *The Wonderful World of Color*. It was a great success and became the longest running prime time television series in history.

One day an idea came to Disney while he sat watching his two daughters play at the park. There should be a place for children and parents to have fun together, he thought. This idea led Disney to create three family parks—Disneyland, Walt Disney World, and EPCOT Center.

"Some luck," George said. "I wish *I* had an imagination!"

"Everyone has an imagination. You just have to learn how to use yours!" someone said.

"What?" George said. "Who said that?" George looked around but didn't see anyone.

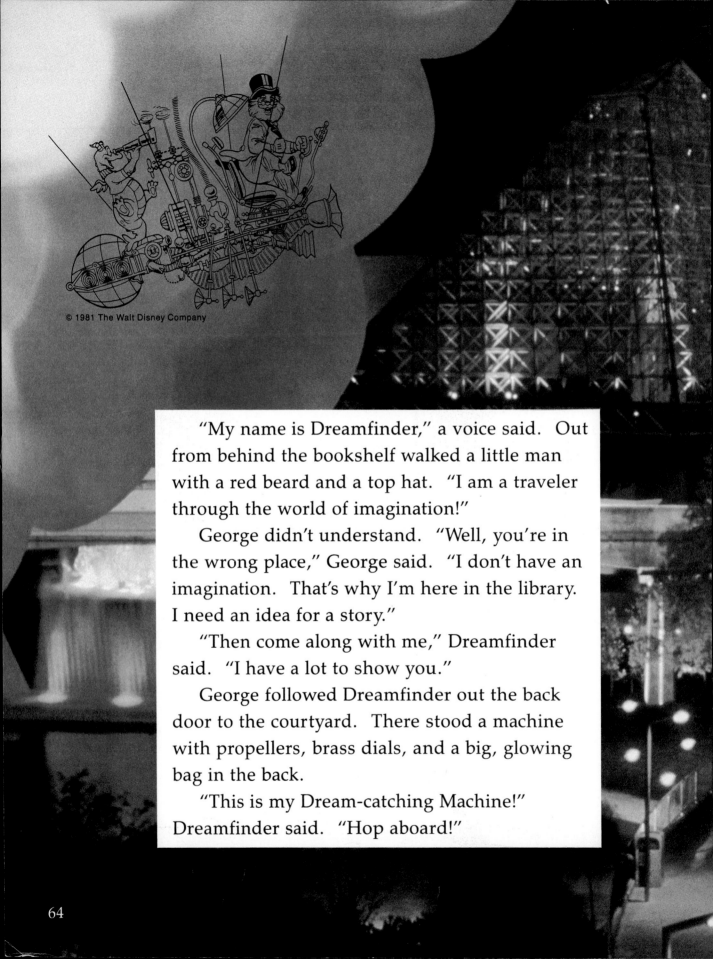

"My name is Dreamfinder," a voice said. Out from behind the bookshelf walked a little man with a red beard and a top hat. "I am a traveler through the world of imagination!"

George didn't understand. "Well, you're in the wrong place," George said. "I don't have an imagination. That's why I'm here in the library. I need an idea for a story."

"Then come along with me," Dreamfinder said. "I have a lot to show you."

George followed Dreamfinder out the back door to the courtyard. There stood a machine with propellers, brass dials, and a big, glowing bag in the back.

"This is my Dream-catching Machine!" Dreamfinder said. "Hop aboard!"

"Oh, I like to fly!" George said. He climbed in and before he knew it, he was up in the air. They circled above the library and then over George's neighborhood. Only seconds later they were heading down toward two glass pyramids.

"Where are we?" George asked.

"This is where I work," Dreamfinder said. "Now get ready for our landing."

They landed with a bump. Then they got out and walked inside one of the pyramids. Next they stepped onto a moving cart.

"Is this some sort of carnival ride?" George asked.

"It's more than just a ride," the little man said. "It's a Journey into Imagination."

George still didn't understand. They moved into a room with overstuffed boxes and drawers.

"This is the Dreamport," Dreamfinder said. "You are sure to find an idea here. Look over there! There's a box filled with winter days. Or go grab some musical notes from that bird cage!"

George looked around the room at all the unusual things.

"Pick out a sound or two from that open drawer! If you listen closely, I think you will hear a dragon's laugh!" Dreamfinder said with a smile.

"I don't believe in dragons," George said.

Dreamfinder started handing things to George. "Take this dragon's laugh, and that crocodile nose. Let's take these big yellow eyes and these pointy horns. While we're at it, let's add these tiny hummingbird wings."

George's arms were full of strange objects. He felt something move. Then suddenly he thought the whole pile was going to fall. He looked again, and there was a little dragon in his arms! "Meet Figment!" said Dreamfinder. The little dragon jumped out of George's arms and flew around the room singing.

"I don't believe it! How did you do it?" George asked.

"You just collect a little idea from here and a little idea from there. Before you know it, you have something new!" Dreamfinder said.

"How can I do that for my homework?" George asked.

"Come and visit what I call the Image Works," Dreamfinder said. "Maybe you will find something interesting there!"

Dreamfinder led George into a big room filled with machines, colors, and sounds. "This is the playground of the imagination," Dreamfinder said. "Here, you can act in your own movie and conduct your own orchestra!"

"I've always wanted to conduct an orchestra," George said. He stood in front of the orchestra, raised his hands to start the opening, and then . . . *Crash!*

"What? Where am I?" George said to himself. "Where's Dreamfinder? And Figment?"

George looked around. He was still on the floor of the library. "I must have fallen asleep. Was my trip just a dream?" he wondered.

George got up and put his book back on the shelf and walked home.

"I still don't have an idea for my story," he told his mother when he got home. Then he told her how he had fallen asleep at the library and dreamed about a trip through two giant pyramids.

"Why, George," his mother said. "That sounds like a ride at EPCOT Center. It's called Journey into Imagination."

"But I've never been to the EPCOT Center," George said. "I've only read about it today in the library."

"Then that's how you imagined it!" his mother said.

"You mean I *do* have an imagination?" George asked.

"Of course you do!" his mother said. "And what an imagination!"

That afternoon George didn't have any problem writing his story. He wrote about his trip with Dreamfinder. As a matter of fact, George couldn't wait to write another story. Now that he had found his imagination, he could take more trips to places he had never been.

Think About It

1. Why was George so certain that his homework would be difficult?
2. How did Walt Disney's interests as a boy turn into his lifetime work?
3. How did Dreamfinder try to prove to George that he did have an imagination?
4. What suggestions do you think George would give to a person who said, "I have no imagination"?

Create and Share   Create a new animal like Figment by putting together parts of different animals. Give your animal a name and tell about its habits.

Explore   Think of a movie or a television program you have watched. How did the writers use their imagination?

NO PETS
ALLOWED
IN ZOO

PATRICK'S DINOSAURS

by Carol Carrick

Patrick and his brother Hank went to the zoo on Saturday. They stood outside a tall fence and watched the elephants.

"I'll bet that elephant is the biggest animal in the whole world," said Patrick.

"You think he's big?" Hank said. "A brontosaurus was heavier than *ten* elephants."

"Gosh!" said Patrick. If Hank said so, it must be true. Hank knew all about dinosaurs. He knew more about everything because he was older and already went to school.

Patrick squeezed his eyes half-shut. What would a dinosaur that weighed as much as ten elephants look like? The brontosaurus he imagined turned and looked right at him.

"Did a brontosaurus eat people?" he asked nervously.

"Just plants," answered Hank.

Patrick's dinosaur started eating leaves from one of the trees.

DO NOT FEED THE ANIMALS

They went to see the crocodiles next. Crocs were Patrick's favorite because he liked to scare himself.

"Those are shrimpy," said Hank. "In the days of dinosaurs, crocodiles grew three times that big."

"Wow!" said Patrick.

"Just their *jaws* were twice as big as you are," added Hank.

Patrick imagined an enormous crocodile. It was three times bigger than the other crocs. It was so big that it wanted the whole pool for itself.

The other crocodiles were too slow getting out. So the enormous crocodile opened its jaws that were twice as big as Patrick and gobbled them all up.

Patrick backed away. "We didn't see the monkeys yet."

When they had seen the monkeys and the seals, Patrick and Hank went for a row on the zoo lake.

Patrick looked down into the deep green water. What was that dark shape next to their boat? "Did dinosaurs know how to swim?" he asked.

"Some did," answered Hank. "Diplodocus, the longest dinosaur, could stay under water like a submarine because its nose was on top of its head."

Patrick was afraid to move. Out of the corner of his eyes he saw the big thing swimming along next to them. It might rise and dump them over!

"What's that!" he cried. "We're going to bump into it!"

"No, dopey. That's just the shadow from our boat," Hank said.

Patrick wasn't so sure. "Let's go home now," he said. "Rowing makes me tired."

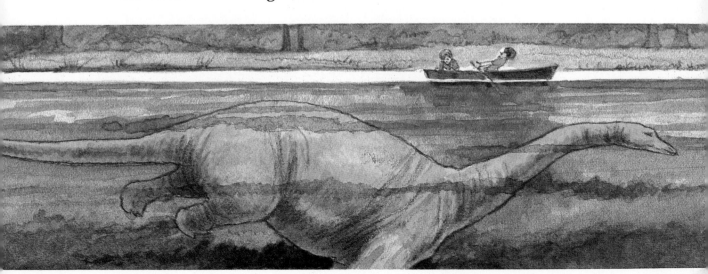

When they got on the bus Patrick felt better, even though Hank was still showing off how much he knew about dinosaurs.

"A stegosaurus was bigger than one of those cars," Hank said. "But its brain was only the size of a walnut."

Patrick looked out the window. In his mind the lane of cars was a line of walnut-brained stegosauruses. The plates on their backs swayed like sails as they plodded along.

Hank reached up and rang the bell for the driver to stop. "A triceratops was tougher than a stegosaurus," he said. "It could even take on a tyrannosaurus."

The bus stopped at their corner. On the other side of the street Patrick thought he saw a triceratops waiting for the traffic light.

When Patrick and his brother climbed down from the bus, the hot, dusty street became a prehistoric forest. Tropical birds screamed a warning. Too late! A tyrannosaurus crashed into the clearing.

Patrick held his breath as the triceratops lowered its huge head. Its horns pointed ahead like three enormous spears. When the traffic light changed, the triceratops charged.

"Run!" Patrick yelled. He headed for their house.

"What's the hurry?" called Hank.

Patrick didn't feel safe until the front door slammed shut. He ran upstairs. He wanted to look out his window, but first he had to ask Hank something.

"How big was a tyrannosaurus?"

"Big," said Hank.

"Up to the second floor, maybe?" asked Patrick.

"At least," Hank agreed.

"That's what I was afraid of," said Patrick. He peeked into his bedroom. Sure enough, the ugly head of the tyrannosaurus almost filled his window.

The dinosaur opened its mouth to show teeth like daggers. Patrick didn't think this dinosaur ate leaves.

"Are you *sure* there are no more dinosaurs around?" he asked Hank.

"Positive. The dinosaurs have been gone for sixty million years."

Patrick gave a sigh of relief. And the dinosaur disappeared.

Think About It

1. What questions would you ask Hank to find out more about dinosaurs?
2. Why was Patrick able to see all the dinosaurs that Hank told him about?
3. Have you ever imagined that something someone told you about was real? What was it?
4. Explain how Patrick's imagination ran away with him.

Create and Share   On a class chart, write a fact that you have learned about dinosaurs.

Explore   Find a book about dinosaurs or look in the encyclopedia for more facts about them. Find out what happened to them.

Meet the Author and the Illustrator: Carol and Donald Carrick

by Meg Buckley

In *Patrick's Dinosaurs*, you read about a boy named Patrick who goes to the zoo with his older brother Hank. On the way home, Patrick imagines dinosaurs coming to life until Hank tells him that they disappeared long ago.

The author of this story is Carol Carrick. Her husband, Donald Carrick, is the illustrator. They have been creating children's stories for over 20 years and have done 32 books together. As soon as Carol finishes writing a story, Donald begins to draw the pictures. Even though Carol writes and Donald draws, they help each other think of ideas.

"Our children were in love with dinosaurs," Carol said. This made the Carricks think a dinosaur story would be fun for children. One night the Carricks went to the movies. On their way home, they saw a construction crane towering over their house. Its long neck made it look like a brontosaurus. Donald wondered about a story in which "dinosaurs could walk down Main Street." That way, children could see how big dinosaurs really were. As you can guess, this is how *Patrick's Dinosaurs* came to be.

The Carricks saw how much children liked their dinosaur book, so they wrote a sequel. A sequel is a story that comes after another story. It has the same characters, but something different happens. Most of the time, the sequel begins where the first story ends.

In the sequel to *Patrick's Dinosaurs*, Patrick uses his imagination to explain to Hank how dinosaurs disappeared. Next you will see what Patrick imagined in *What Happened to Patrick's Dinosaurs?*

What Happened to Patrick's Dinosaurs?

by Carol Carrick

Patrick was helping his big brother, Hank, rake leaves.

"Where did they go?" asked Patrick.

"Who?" asked Hank.

"Dinosaurs, of course." Patrick never talked about anything else.

"Well, some people think the world got too hot for dinosaurs," said Hank. "And some think it got too cold. Maybe an asteroid hit the earth and covered it with dust." He showered Patrick with a pile of leaves.

"That's not what *I* think," said Patrick.

"And what do you think?" asked his brother.

"I think that, once upon a time, dinosaurs and people were friends," said Patrick.

"There weren't any people then," said Hank. "Cave men came much later."

"The people didn't live in caves," said Patrick. "Dinosaurs built them cozy houses."

"I suppose there were dinosaur houses, too," said Hank.

"That's silly," said Patrick. "Dinosaurs didn't live in houses. They just made them."

81

Hank smiled. "What happened when the dinosaurs got hungry?" he asked.

"They knocked down trees and planted bananas," said Patrick. "And they always shared. Can I have a bite?"

"Then dinosaurs invented cars," said Patrick, "because people couldn't run as fast as they could."

"Dinosaurs made cars?" said Hank. "Why not airplanes?"

"They did make airplanes," said Patrick. "And they made roads for people to drive on. Dinosaurs were big and strong so they did all the work."

"If they did everything, what were the people doing all this time?" asked Hank.

"Oh, they got very bored," said Patrick. "So dinosaurs put on shows, to make them happy. Some of the smart people learned to do tricks."

"Dinosaurs taught *people* tricks?"

"Dinosaurs wanted to teach people how everything works," explained Patrick. "But people were only interested in recess and lunch."

Hank lay down on a pile of leaves. Patrick lay down, too. "Guess what happened then," Patrick said.

"I give up."

"Dinosaurs got tired of doing all the work," said Patrick. "And nobody would help them. So they built a big spaceship and left."

"Dinosaurs couldn't fit in a spaceship," said Hank.

"Then how could they leave?" asked Patrick.

"I didn't say they left," Hank said.

"But they did," said Patrick. "And they never came back. After a while people forgot that there ever were dinosaurs. They had to take care of themselves now, and they didn't know how."

It grew dark and the first stars came out.
Hank and Patrick watched as one bright star
moved across the sky.

"You really think dinosaurs are out there?"
asked Hank.

Patrick nodded. "But they miss us," he said.
"And every so often they check to see how we're
doing."

Think About It

1. How did imagination help Carol and Donald Carrick write "Patrick's Dinosaurs" and its sequel?
2. What reasons did Hank give for why there are no dinosaurs left?
3. What was Patrick's explanation?
4. Why might Patrick make a good author some day?
5. What are some of the different ways the characters in this cluster used their imagination?

Create and Share   Write a sequel to the sequel! Patrick says that the dinosaurs check on people every so often to see how they are doing. In your sequel, have the dinosaurs come back from space. Describe what happens next.

Explore   The Carricks have written many other books. Visit the library and find another one to read.

One picture is worth more than ten thousand words.

Chinese proverb

Click !

A Very Strange Photo

by Stephen Mooser

One day Marcella went to the bake shop to pick up a pie for her father. She stopped to read a big sign in the window.

"I'd like to win that trip," thought Marcella. "After I pick up Papa's pie, I'll go home and take some pictures."

When Marcella got home, she saw her friend Alfredo. He was standing near a tree with a sheet over his head.

"Boo!" said Alfredo. "I'm a ghost!"

"Don't boo at me," Marcella said, laughing. "You're not a ghost. You're Alfredo."

"You mean you're not afraid? I didn't scare you?" asked Alfredo.

"No, but you did give me an idea," said Marcella. "How would you like me to take your picture?"

"I'd like that," said Alfredo, "but why do you want my picture?"

"The Best Bake Shop is giving a prize to the person who takes the oddest picture," said Marcella. "A photo of a ghost would be quite strange."

All that day, Marcella took pictures of Alfredo.
She had him lie on his front and then lie on his
back. She had him jump over the gate. She had
him juggle with some sticks.

"These pictures should be great!" said
Marcella when she was done with the roll.
"What could be stranger than a ghost who can
jump and juggle? One of my pictures is sure to
win the prize."

The next day, Marcella went to see her friend
Edward. She thought he'd be just the person to
develop and print her special pictures. "Can you
print some pictures for me?" asked Marcella. "I
need them by Monday."

"You can have them first thing Monday
morning," said Edward.

"Do a good job," said Marcella. "If these
pictures turn out well, I'll win a trip to the city."

"I'll do my best," said Edward.

Early Monday morning, Marcella got a phone call from Edward. "I'm afraid I have some bad news," he said. "Your pictures didn't come out. It's all my fault. I did something wrong. I'm very sorry. If you take some more pictures, I'll develop and print them right away."

"There isn't time," said Marcella, shaking her head as she put down the phone.

Just then Alfredo came in. "What's wrong?" he asked.

"The pictures didn't turn out," said Marcella. "Now I won't win that trip."

"Maybe it's not as bad as it sounds," said Alfredo. "Let's go over to Edward's house and look at the photos. Maybe one of them came out."

When they got to Edward's house, he handed them the pictures. Not one had turned out. Each looked like a field of snow. At first, Marcella felt very sad. But the more she looked at the photos, the better she felt. At last, she smiled and said, "With luck, these photos may win first prize."

"How can these photos win anything?" asked Alfredo. "There's nothing on them."

"I think you're wrong," said Marcella. "There's plenty on them. Come on! Let's go to the bake shop."

Alfredo and Edward had no idea what
Marcella was talking about. But they said they'd
go anyway. When they reached the bake shop,
Marcella printed something at the bottom of one
photo. Then she stuck it on the wall next to
some other pictures.

After a while, a man in a red tie came by and
looked at all the pictures on the wall. When he
saw Marcella's picture, he smiled.

"I think he likes it," said Marcella.

"No, he's laughing at it," said Alfredo. "After
all, it's just white paper."

Before long, the man in the red tie took down Marcella's photo. Then he walked to the front of the shop.

"Marcella's picture wins a special prize," he said. "I've never seen a stranger picture."

Alfredo couldn't believe his ears. "What's so strange about a piece of white paper?" he asked.

"Go over and look at it," said Marcella. "You will see that it is more than just a piece of white paper."

Alfredo went over and looked. When he saw what Marcella had printed, he knew why the man had picked her photo.

Photo of a ghost looking for a sheet in a snowstorm.

Think About It

1. Why did Marcella want to take pictures of Alfredo?
2. Did Marcella make a good choice when she asked Edward to develop her pictures? Explain.
3. How did Marcella use her imagination to win a prize?
4. Do you think it was right that Marcella's photo won a prize? Why or why not?

Create and Share   Write some new titles for Marcella's photo. Share your titles with your classmates.

Explore   Look at some books or magazines that show photos. Try to find out who took them. Pick a photo that you would like to use in the Best Bake Shop contest.

FuNNY PHoToGRaPHS

by Janet Hurwitz

Here's how to use pictures from magazines to make funny photographs.

THINGS YOU WILL NEED

Magazines	Paste
Scissors	Heavy construction paper

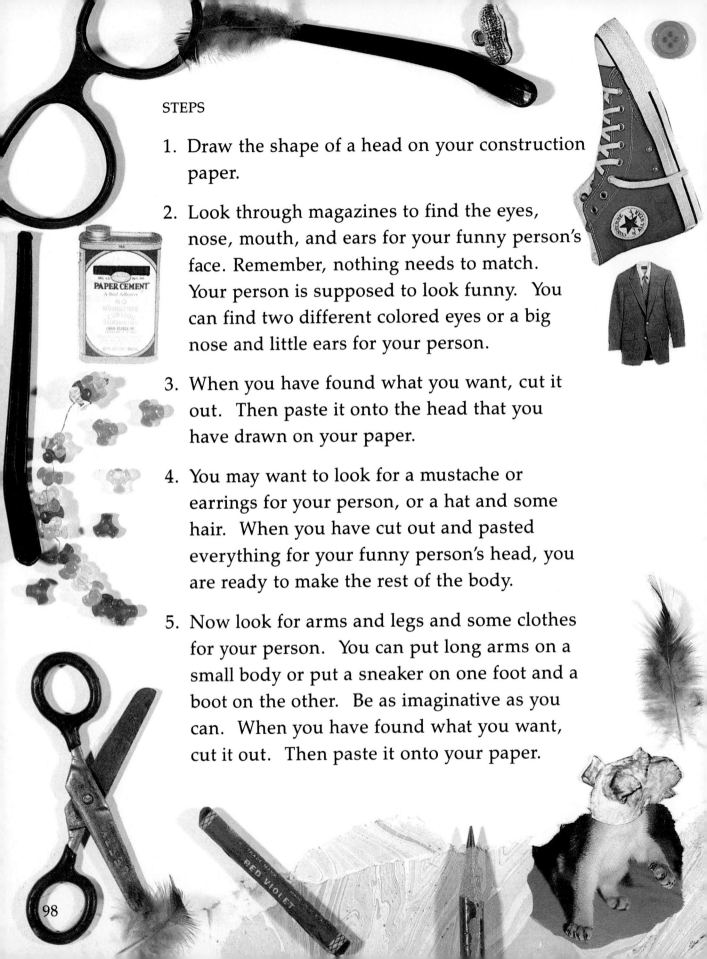

STEPS

1. Draw the shape of a head on your construction paper.

2. Look through magazines to find the eyes, nose, mouth, and ears for your funny person's face. Remember, nothing needs to match. Your person is supposed to look funny. You can find two different colored eyes or a big nose and little ears for your person.

3. When you have found what you want, cut it out. Then paste it onto the head that you have drawn on your paper.

4. You may want to look for a mustache or earrings for your person, or a hat and some hair. When you have cut out and pasted everything for your funny person's head, you are ready to make the rest of the body.

5. Now look for arms and legs and some clothes for your person. You can put long arms on a small body or put a sneaker on one foot and a boot on the other. Be as imaginative as you can. When you have found what you want, cut it out. Then paste it onto your paper.

6. If you want, you can make an unusual background for your person. You can put your person in a snowy mountain scene if it is wearing a bathing suit. Or you can put your person in the desert if it is wearing a heavy coat. These are just some ideas, but you can think of more.

99

7. Now you can add extras to your funny
   photograph. You can make your person
   do something unusual or you can put
   funny objects in the photograph. Your person
   could be walking an unusual pet. Maybe it
   could be wearing fruit on its head. There are
   many different things you can do with your
   photograph. No two pictures will ever be alike.

8. If you want, you can think of a title for your
   photograph. You can even write a story for it.
   When you are finished, you can hang your
   funny photograph up on your wall.

Think About It

1. What are the steps in putting together funny photographs?
2. What things other than people might make good subjects for a funny photograph?
3. Do you think anyone can make a funny photograph? Explain.

Explore   Look through magazines to find some photographs.

Create and Share   Cut out the photographs you found in magazines. Paste them on paper and make up some crazy titles or captions for them.

Simple Pictures Are Best

by Nancy Willard

The shoemaker and his wife lived in a small house so far from other houses that their road seemed the last road in the world.

"Everything we want is here," said the shoemaker.

Behind the house they planted a garden. The sunflowers grew right up to the roof, and a squash grew fat and ripe as a pig.

A one-eyed cat arrived one day, caught all the mice in the house, and stayed.

During the day the shoemaker worked at his bench and made up poems.

His wife Ellen painted pictures and baked pies.

They both worked in the garden.

In the evening the shoemaker played the fiddle and his wife played the spoons while the shoemaker sang,

> *"The little black bull come down the meadow,*
> *Hoosen Johnny, Hoosen Johnny,*
> *The little black bull come down the meadow*
> *Long time ago."*

One day Ellen said, "Tomorrow is our wedding anniversary. I would like to have our picture taken."

So the shoemaker called a photographer, and the photographer arrived with a camera so large that a dozen swallows could have nested in it.

Behind the photographer walked a little boy
holding a camera case.

"James," said the photographer, "hand me my
film."

So James opened the camera case and took out
some film. The photographer put the film into
the camera. Then he put the camera on a tripod.

"I'm ready," said the photographer. "Where
would you like the picture taken?"

"In front of the house," said the shoemaker.

"In the garden," said Ellen, "to show off our
squash."

One said yes and the other said no, and so it
went until James said, "Why don't you pick the
squash and put the squash in the picture and take
the picture in front of the house?"

So the shoemaker and his wife went into the garden and picked the squash, and together they carried it out of the garden. Then they sat down in their chairs in front of the house.

But no sooner had Ellen sat down than she jumped up again.

"If we're going to put the squash in the picture, we should put the carrots in it, too. They're much prettier than the squash."

"Simple pictures are best," said the photographer.

But Ellen had already run off to fetch the carrots.

When she returned, the photographer said, "Madam, what clothes will you be wearing for the picture?"

Now Ellen did not want to admit that she was, at that moment, wearing her best dress. So she said, "I shall wear my blue hat."

"I like your red hat better," said the shoemaker.

One said yes and the other said no, and so it went until James said, "Why doesn't Ellen wear the blue hat and the shoemaker wear the red one?"

"Simple pictures are best," warned the photographer.

But the shoemaker had already run off to fetch the hats.

When he returned, the photographer said, "Shoemaker, what shoes will you be wearing for the picture?"

Now the shoemaker did not want to admit that, though he made shoes, he never wore them.

"My old shoes," said the shoemaker.

"I like the new ones best," said Ellen.

One said yes and the other said no, and so it went until James said, "Why don't you wear the old ones on your feet and the new ones on your ears?"

"Simple pictures are best," warned the photographer.

But the shoemaker had already run off to fetch the shoes.

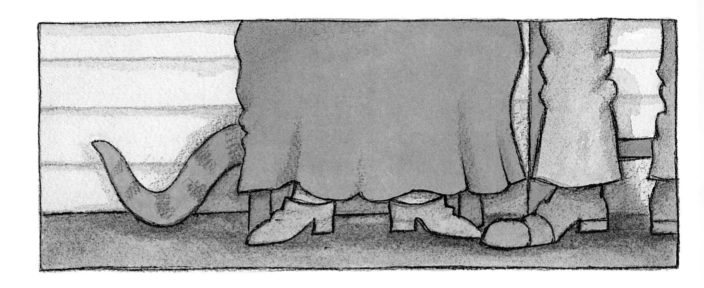

When he returned, he was wearing his old
shoes on his feet and his new shoes on his ears
and the red hat on his head, and he sat down,
with the squash in his lap, next to Ellen in her
blue hat, with the carrots in her lap, in front of
the house.

The photographer threw a black cloth over the
camera and put his head under it.

"We're ready," said Ellen. "What's wrong?"

"Madam, you have a tail under your chair,"
said the photographer in a muffled voice.

"Meow!" said the chair.

"Why it's the cat," exclaimed Ellen, and
reaching under her chair, she brought out the
one-eyed cat. "If we're going to put the squash
and the carrots in the picture, we must have the
cat in it, too. She's much prettier than the squash
and the carrots."

"Simple pictures are best," warned the photographer.

The cat sat down between the shoemaker, wearing his old shoes on his feet and his new shoes on his ears and the red hat on his head with the squash in his lap, and Ellen, in her blue hat with the carrots in her lap, in front of the house.

The photographer threw his black cloth over the camera and crawled under it again.

"We're ready," said the shoemaker. "What's wrong?"

"Shoemaker, you keep moving your hands," said the photographer in a muffled voice.

"I don't know what to do with them," said the shoemaker with a sigh. "I'm not comfortable without my fiddle."

"Well, then, get your fiddle," said James.

"Simple pictures are best," warned the photographer.

But the shoemaker had already run off to fetch his fiddle.

When he returned, holding his fiddle and wearing his old shoes on his feet and his new shoes on his ears and the red hat on his head, he sat down, with the squash in his lap, next to Ellen in her blue hat with the carrots in her lap, and the cat sat between them in front of the house.

The photographer threw his black cloth over the camera and crawled under it.

"We're ready," said Ellen. "What's wrong?"

"Madam, you keep moving *your* hands," said the photographer in a muffled voice.

"I don't know what to do with them," said Ellen with a sigh. "I must hold something, too. I shall hold my spoons."

"Your spoons!" exclaimed the shoemaker. "That will look odd unless you're holding a dish as well. You can hold the spoons and the blueberry pie you baked this morning."

"Simple pictures are best," warned the photographer.

But Ellen had already run off to fetch her spoons and pie.

When she returned, she sat down, in her blue hat with the carrots in her lap and her spoons in her hand and her blueberry pie in her arms, next to the shoemaker, holding his fiddle and wearing his old shoes on his feet and his new shoes on his ears and the red hat on his head with the squash in his lap, and the cat sat between them in front of the house.

But no sooner had she sat down than she jumped up again.

"I don't want people to think I do nothing but bake pies. I shall put one of my paintings in the picture as well."

"Simple pictures are best," warned the photographer.

But Ellen had already run off to fetch her painting.

When she returned, she leaned it against her chair.

The photographer threw his black cloth over the camera and crawled under it once more.

"We're ready," said the shoemaker and his wife. "What's wrong?"

"Smile," said the photographer.

"I can't," said Ellen.

"I can't either," said the shoemaker.

So James ran into the garden and picked half a
dozen turnips and ran back to the photographer
and began to juggle with the turnips.

"Ha," said the shoemaker.

"Ho," said his wife.

But they did not smile.

Then James ran into the kitchen and fetched a
giant frying pan and ran back to the
photographer and stood on his head in the frying
pan while juggling the turnips.

"Ha hum," said the shoemaker.

"Ho ha," said his wife.

But they did not smile.

Then James ran into the orchard and gathered a dozen apples. He did not see the bull browsing under the tree until the bull made a hideous noise. James dropped the apples and ran back to the photographer. The bull did not see James, but he *did* see the photographer.

"Ha, ha, ha!" laughed the shoemaker and his wife.

And James clicked the shutter.

Then the shoemaker and his wife jumped to their feet and caught the bull, tied him up, and helped the photographer to a chair.

"When will the picture be ready?" asked Ellen.

The photographer looked at his watch.

"Not long. It's developing right now."

In half a minute the photographer took out the film and opened it. They all looked.

The photographer sighed. "Simple pictures are best."

PUNIDDLES

from the book by Bruce and Brett McMillan

pun · id · dle (pŭn · ĭd´ · l)

n. l. A pair of photographs that suggest an obvious solution to figuring out compound words in a punny way.
[Source: pun, riddle]

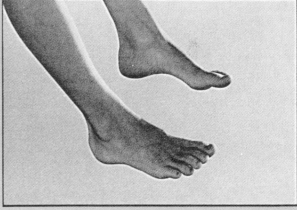

BARE FEET

HOME RUN

PINEAPPLES

TOADSTOOLS

RAINBOWS

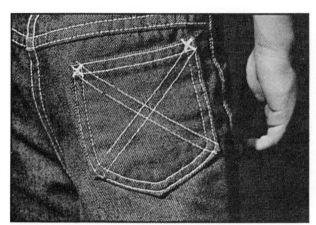

POCKETBOOKS

BOTTLE CAPS

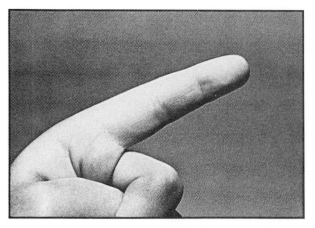

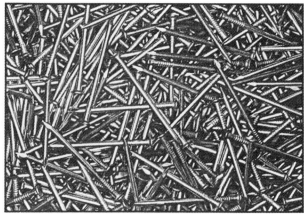

FINGERNAILS

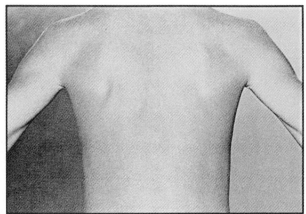

PIGGYBACK

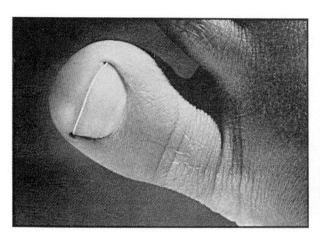

TOW TRUCKS

EYEGLASSES

 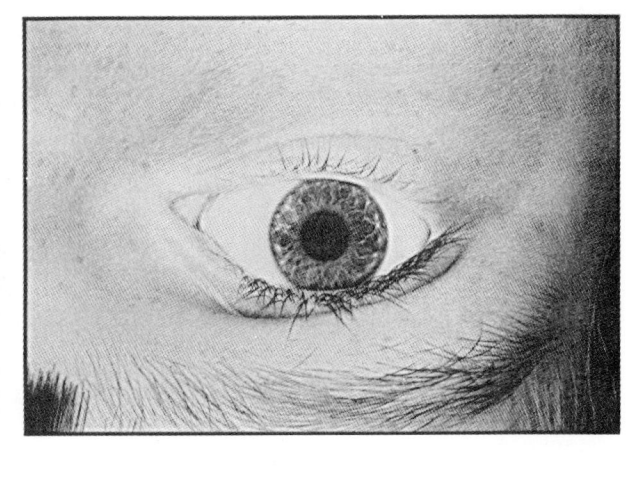

DOGCATCHER

FOOTSTEPS

 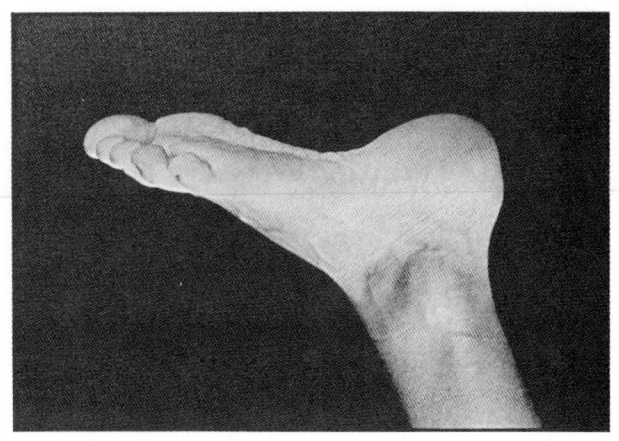

HORSESHOES

COWBOYS

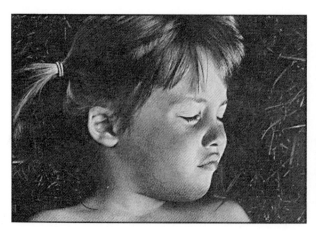

SLEEPING BAGS

Think About It

1. Why did the photographer keep saying, "Simple pictures are best"?
2. What do you think was the funniest thing that the shoemaker and Ellen had in their photograph? Tell why you think so.
3. Tell how you think the photographer came up with the idea of puniddles.
4. Why do you think people often act so silly when it's time to have their picture taken?

Create and Share   List at least four important things to remember when taking a picture. Compare your list with a friend's.

Explore   Check the encyclopedia or find a book at the library that describes how pictures are developed.

What Will I Wear?

Where does a sheep get his wool cut?

At a baa baa shop

Where do frogs hang up their coats?

In the croak room

When I go into the jungle, how will I be able to spot a leopard?

You won't. The leopards will already be spotted.

Greedy Zebra

by Mwenye Hadithi

Long, long ago, all the animals in the world were a dull, depressing color. They had no coats, no horns, no spots, and no stripes. They were just dull and dusty. Until . . .

One stormy day in the heart of the leafy forests of Africa there was a great rumbling in the earth. All of a sudden a huge cave appeared in the ground. A few of the animals crept up to this new and wonderful sight. When the bravest of them looked into the darkness she saw something glittering among the rocks.

The cave was full of furs and skins, all glossy and new! Stepping inside, she came across horns and tails of countless shapes and sizes, and needles, and threads of a thousand different colors. Trembling with excitement, she rushed out to tell the other animals what she had seen.

The news spread far and wide. Soon all the animals were on their way to see the cave, running and jumping and sliding and swinging, and slithering through the trees.

All, that is, except one—Greedy Zebra. Greedy Zebra never ever stopped eating. He certainly wasn't going to give up a single mouthful for a silly old cave of any sort.

"Lots of time to go visiting caves," said Greedy Zebra. He stuffed grass into his mouth. "Plenty of time," he said.

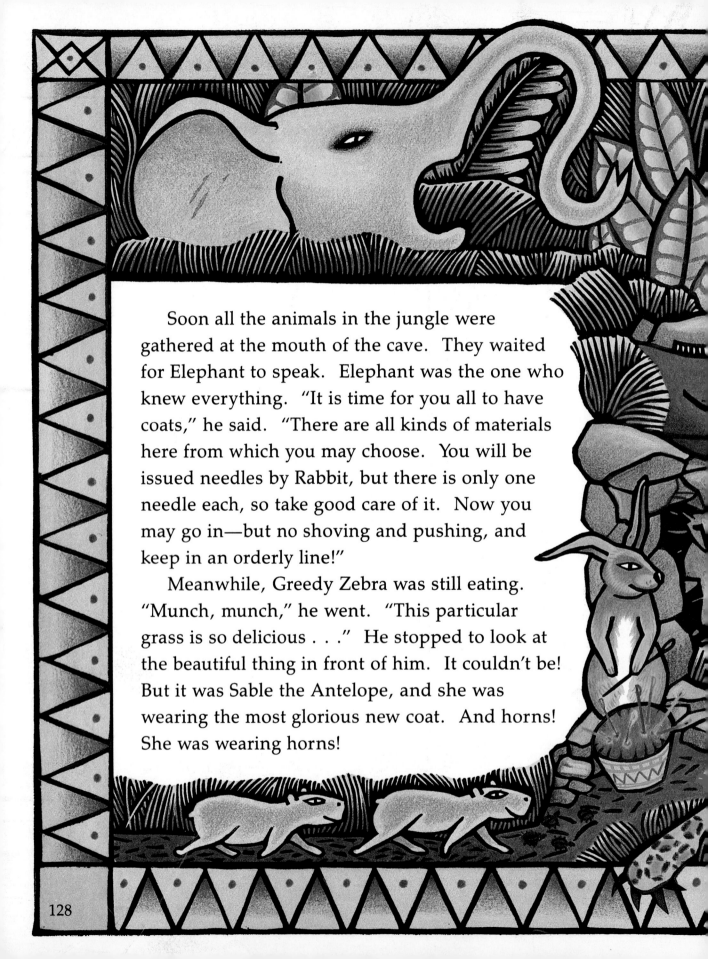

Soon all the animals in the jungle were gathered at the mouth of the cave. They waited for Elephant to speak. Elephant was the one who knew everything. "It is time for you all to have coats," he said. "There are all kinds of materials here from which you may choose. You will be issued needles by Rabbit, but there is only one needle each, so take good care of it. Now you may go in—but no shoving and pushing, and keep in an orderly line!"

Meanwhile, Greedy Zebra was still eating. "Munch, munch," he went. "This particular grass is so delicious . . ." He stopped to look at the beautiful thing in front of him. It couldn't be! But it was Sable the Antelope, and she was wearing the most glorious new coat. And horns! She was wearing horns!

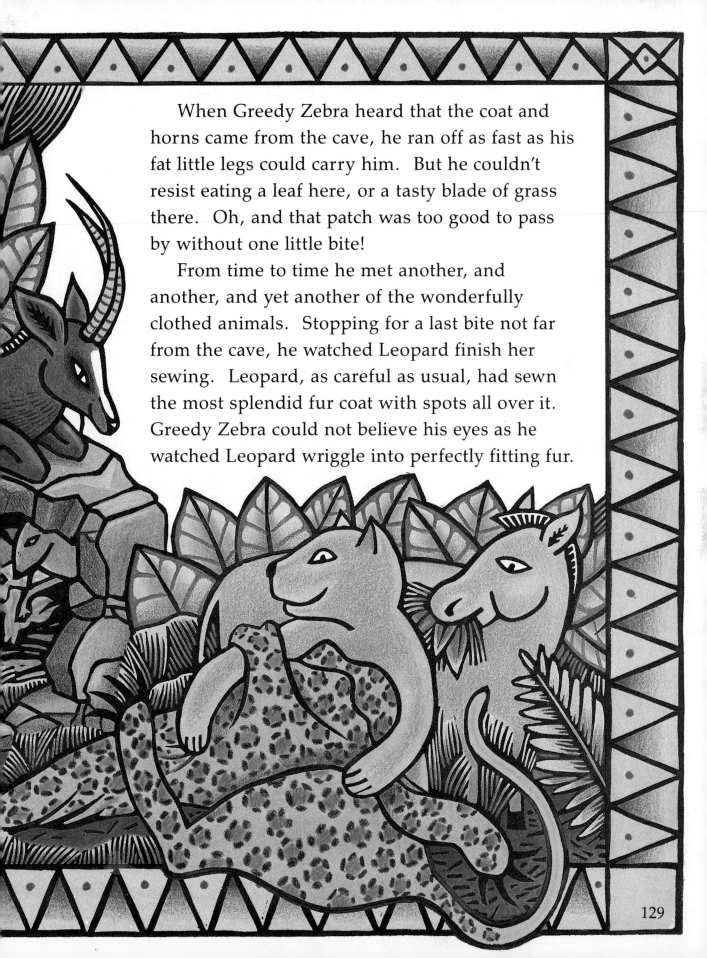

When Greedy Zebra heard that the coat and horns came from the cave, he ran off as fast as his fat little legs could carry him. But he couldn't resist eating a leaf here, or a tasty blade of grass there. Oh, and that patch was too good to pass by without one little bite!

From time to time he met another, and another, and yet another of the wonderfully clothed animals. Stopping for a last bite not far from the cave, he watched Leopard finish her sewing. Leopard, as careful as usual, had sewn the most splendid fur coat with spots all over it. Greedy Zebra could not believe his eyes as he watched Leopard wriggle into perfectly fitting fur.

"I shall have spots like that," Greedy Zebra
said to himself. Then he hurried off,
eager to reach the cave.

But it was a hot day, so he stopped for a cool
drink at a stream, and there he came across a
patch of the greenest grass he had ever seen.

"Delicious," he munched, smacking his
chubby lips.

Back at the cave most of the animals were
leaving. Only Rhino and Elephant were still
cutting their material. They had chosen a very
strong gray cloth. Poor old Rhino, who couldn't
see very well, had stuck his horns on any old way
and was having a terrible time. He was too
nervous to ask Elephant for help, because he
knew Elephant would only make fun of him.
Rhino had dropped his needle, and the more he
searched, the further into the bushes he kicked it.
Finally, he put on the baggy coat, and shuffled off
in a very bad mood.

Just then Greedy Zebra trotted by, with blades of grass bulging from his mouth. "I'll have spots like Leopard," he was saying, "and horns like Antelope, a mane like Lion, and a tail like Leopard. I shall be the finest-looking animal in the forest!"

At the risk of indigestion, he gave a short gallop into the cave. Then he stopped.

There was nothing left! No horns, no fine cloth—nothing. He searched through the cave, but all he could find were a few strips of black material. He cut them all to the same size and stitched them together.

"It looks very tight," he thought nervously to himself. Being such a very fat zebra, he had a terrible time squeezing into his coat. He pushed and grunted and oohed and aahed and—pop, he was inside it. But what a tight fit! It was nearly bursting at the seams around his fat tummy. He trotted down to the stream to take a quick bite of a leafy bush—and POP! his coat burst open.

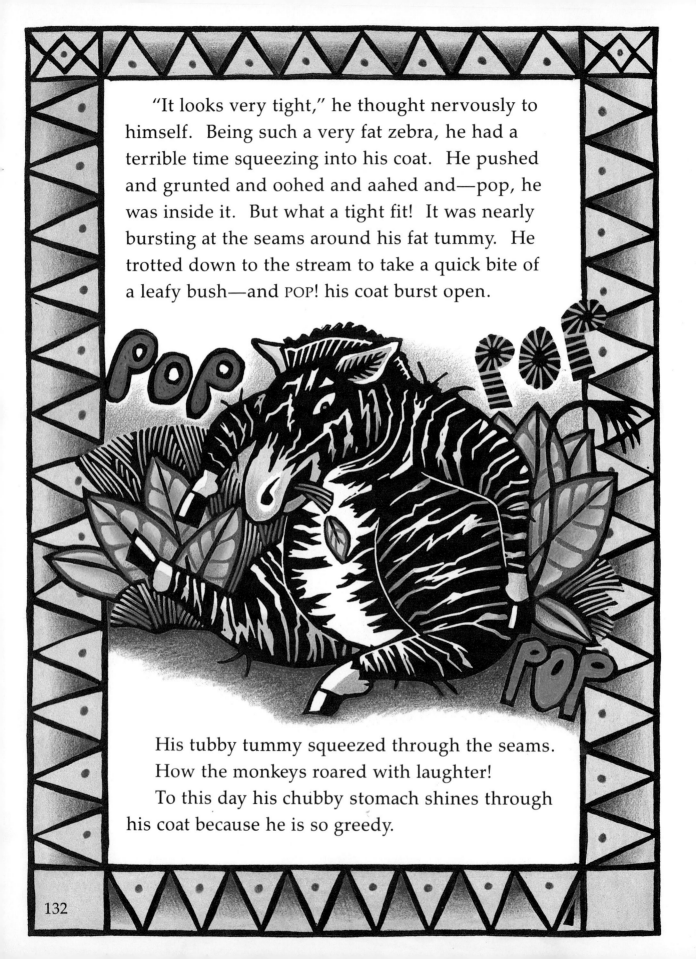

His tubby tummy squeezed through the seams.
How the monkeys roared with laughter!
To this day his chubby stomach shines through his coat because he is so greedy.

Animals Should Definitely Not Wear Clothing

by Judi and Ron Barrett

BECAUSE A SNAKE WOULD LOSE IT

BECAUSE IT WOULD ALWAYS BE WET ON A WALRUS

BECAUSE A KANGAROO WOULD FIND IT QUITE UNNECESSARY

134

BECAUSE A GIRAFFE MIGHT LOOK SORT OF SILLY

BECAUSE OPOSSUMS MIGHT WEAR IT UPSIDE DOWN BY MISTAKE

BECAUSE A MOOSE COULD NEVER MANAGE

AND MOST OF ALL, BECAUSE IT MIGHT BE VERY EMBARRASSING

Animal Camouflage

by Meg Buckley

Did you ever wonder why a tiger has stripes or why a polar bear is all white? This is so they will match their surroundings and other animals will not see them. This is called camouflage. Camouflage helps to keep an animal safe because enemy animals cannot see it well. Camouflage also lets animals get close to their prey so that they can catch food more easily.

The brown and black coloring of the tiger looks much like the colors of the jungle. Even the vertical stripes of the tiger match the tall grass it walks through. Polar bears live in cold, snowy places. The white coat on a polar bear blends into the snow, making it easy for the bear to hide.

There are other animals that use color as camouflage too. Frogs and toads look a lot like their surroundings. Frogs are usually a green color to match the water they swim in. Toads are usually a speckled brown to match the dry ground they hop around on.

Some animals can change from one color to another. The stoat, a type of weasel, is white in the winter to match the snow but brown in the summer to match the dry grass.

The most popular animal known for changing its color is the chameleon, a type of lizard. It changes fast—in about two minutes. Not only does a chameleon change its color to match its surroundings, but it changes color according to how it feels. A chameleon that is angry will turn a dark color, and a scared chameleon will turn white.

Sometimes the shape of an animal will help to hide it. The wandering leaf insect is a good name for a type of insect from Malaysia. It looks just like a leaf. When it is sitting on a real leaf, it is very difficult to see.

The sargassum fish looks like a piece of seaweed. It swims near seaweed so other fish won't see it. When smaller fish swim by, the sargassum fish eats them up.

There is also a type of saltwater snail called the Venus's-comb, whose shell looks like the bones of a dead fish. Fish that like to eat snails pass by the Venus's-comb without thinking there is any food there.

There are some unusual things animals can do to camouflage themselves. The armadillo uses its bone-plated back as armor and rolls up into a ball when it is scared. It does not look much like an animal when it does this. Both the porcupine and the pangolin do the same thing. Instead of a bone-plated back to protect it though, the porcupine has sharp quills that stick up like needles. And the pangolin has hundreds of hard scales that cover its whole body.

A turtle can make itself look different too. When a turtle is in danger, it cannot run away because it is too slow. Instead, it hides in its shell and hopes that another animal will think it is a rock.

Almost all animals use some form of camouflage. Their color or their shape may help them hide. Or they may do something to make themselves look different, like the armadillo. An animal needs to protect itself. Otherwise, it would soon die, it would not be able to catch enough food, or it would be caught *as* food by other animals.

Think About It

1. What is camouflage and why do animals use it?
2. Which animal's camouflage did you find most interesting? Explain why.
3. What problem did the different animals have with wearing clothes in "Animals Should Definitely Not Wear Clothing"?

Create and Share
Imagine that you are an animal being hunted by another animal. Draw a picture of how you would use camouflage. Describe your picture to a friend.

Explore
Pick an animal. Find information in the library that tells how that animal protects itself.

THE ARMADILLO

by Neli Garrido de Rodríguez

They say that the armadillo was a weaver before being the animal it is today. The armadillo had been a weaver for a long time and had become very lazy. It was the weaver's lazy way that changed him into an armadillo.

One day the weaver slowly got the loom ready to weave. Then he put the woolen threads in place and began. After a little while, he stopped working.

"I'll start again tomorrow," he said.

Days passed before he remembered to start working again. He sat in front of the loom. Slowly he passed one thread between the threads of the warp. Then he started getting sleepy. That's the way it always was with the weaver.

One pass of the shuttle, then ten naps. One pass, ten naps.

"What a pity! He's a very good weaver, but so lazy!" said the people in the town.

Winter came. The first winds and frosts let everyone know that it was going to be a very cold one.

All the people got ready for the cold winter weather. They made sure they had clothes to keep them warm. It was then that the weaver realized that he didn't have any heavy clothes to wear.

"Brrr, brrr! And me without a poncho," he said. "What am I going to do? Well, I'm going to have to weave one for myself."

This meant that he would have to sit in front of the loom for several days, weaving and weaving. Just thinking about that made the weaver feel tired.

But he set up the loom anyway. Then he got the thread ready and started working.

At first, everything went very well. One row, another row, tighten the threads. One row, another row, and another and another . . .

When he had made one strip of cloth, he stopped to look at it. The weave was even and tight. It was a weaving so perfect that even he was surprised to see it.

Then he thought he would rest a little while, so he fell asleep. Soon he woke up. How cold it was!

"All right. I have no choice but to keep on weaving," said the weaver as he went back to the loom.

One row, another row. One row, another one, and another . . .

He had not made another full strip when—
sure enough!—he was tired again. But the cold
grew more and more bitter, so there was no time
to rest.

"I have to finish it, or I'll freeze for sure!" said
the weaver.

He sat there weaving and weaving, weaving
and weaving, wea . . . ving . . . and . . . wea . . .

He was tired, but he saw all he had left to do.
"I am freezing, but I'm not finished yet!" he
yelled.

The weaver kept weaving. He had to finish
quickly, so he began to make the weaving very
loose. By weaving loosely, it took less time. The
strips of loose cloth had big gaps between the
threads.

Then the weaver used the threads that were
much thicker and less twisted. Of course, this
made the weave become more loose.

"If I keep on this way, I'm not going to cover
anything!" he said.

So the weaver worked harder and made the
weave tighter. He made the last strips even and
close like the first ones.

Finally he finished and put on the poncho he
had worked so hard to make.

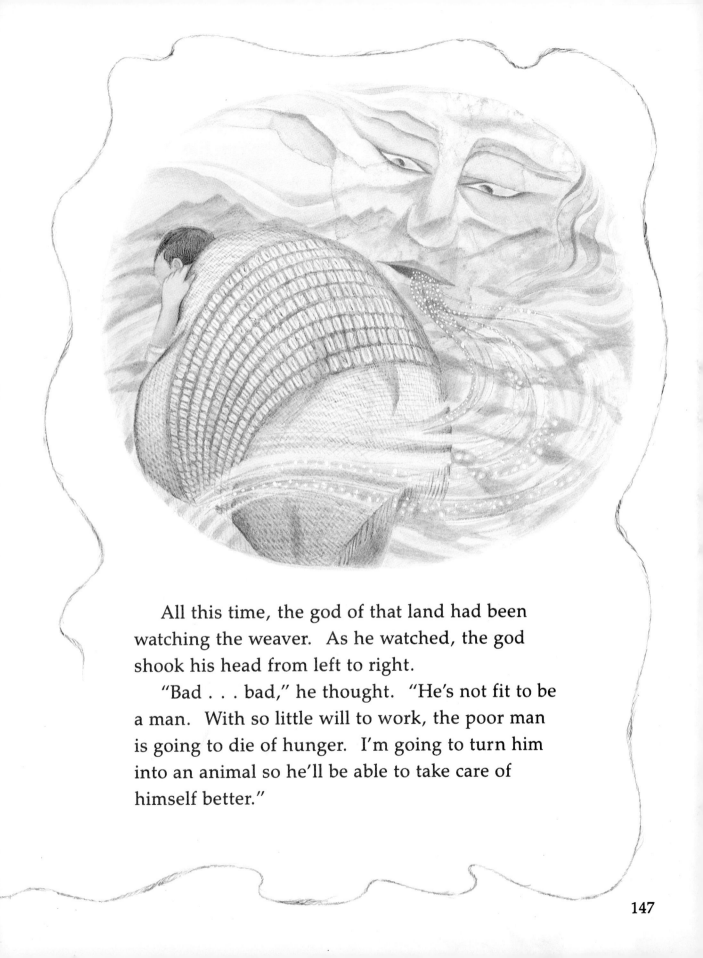

All this time, the god of that land had been watching the weaver. As he watched, the god shook his head from left to right.

"Bad . . . bad," he thought. "He's not fit to be a man. With so little will to work, the poor man is going to die of hunger. I'm going to turn him into an animal so he'll be able to take care of himself better."

No sooner had the god said this than it was
done. The weaver was changed into an
armadillo. The poncho became a shell to protect
the armadillo from bad weather. On each end of
the shell there were plates that were close
together and even. In the middle were large,
separate ones. The pattern of the shell looked
just like that of the poncho the weaver had
hurried to finish.

Think About It

1. What was the weaver's problem?
2. Did the weaver deserve what happened to him? Tell why or why not.
3. What lesson do you think the author of this story wanted the reader to learn?
4. What other story in WHAT WILL I WEAR? is like "The Armadillo"? In what way are these stories alike?

Create and Share   Imagine that you could turn into any animal. What animal would you choose? Draw a picture showing yourself as the animal. Then write a paragraph about why you picked this animal.

Explore   What other story have you heard or read that tells about a person that turns into an animal? Find it, read it again, and share it with your class.

THE ANIMALS COVER UP

by Stephen Krensky

One gray afternoon the animals gathered down at the river for a drink. Some of them had come with their friends. Others had come alone.

The lion roared as he looked at himself in the water. "What a great mane I have," he said.

He looked around proudly. Everyone was watching him, everyone except a turtle crawling along the shore.

The lion stuck his nose in the turtle's path. "Here now," he said, flicking his tail back and forth. "Did you hear what I just said?"

"I think everyone heard you," said the turtle.

"Oh," said the lion. "I thought you weren't paying attention." He smiled at the turtle. "So what do you think of my mane?"

The turtle could see all the lion's big teeth. "It looks good on you," she said wisely.

The lion nodded. "Of course," he said. "It's thick and very handsome."

He moved his head to let the turtle pass.

The elephant snorted. Few animals would dare snort at a lion, but the elephant was big enough to do as she pleased.

"I don't know, Lion," she said. "All that hair must get tangled up. It's hard to keep clean, I suppose. I'd rather have thick skin and as little hair as possible."

She stuck her foot down in the water, splashing the turtle's nose.

"What do you say to that, Turtle?" the elephant asked.

The turtle looked up and up and up at the elephant. "Oh, yes," she said. "Long hair would definitely look strange on your trunk."

"Exactly," said the elephant, backing up onto dry ground.

Two snakes hissed at the elephant.

"Thick skin is so difficult," said one snake.

"I know," said the other. "It is tough and it wrinkles easily."

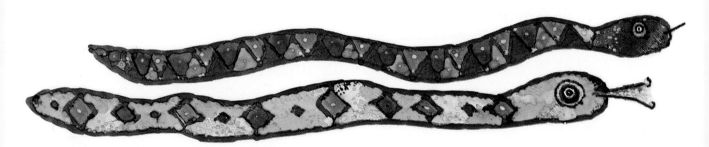

The snakes slithered forward and surrounded the turtle.

"Our skin is smooth," said one snake. "We can twist and ripple across the ground. We never get caught on anything."

"What do you think of that, Turtle?" asked the other snake.

The turtle looked from snake to snake. "I'm sure smooth skin can come in very handy," she said. "I don't do much twisting myself."

"Too bad," said one snake, slithering off to a rock.

"Everybody can't be as lucky as we are," said the other, slithering off as well.

The turtle took a step forward as the bear yawned and said, "Snake skin may be flexible but my thick, soft fur will keep me warm. Besides, you snakes have to grow a new skin every year. That sounds uncomfortable. My fur will last me a lifetime."

The bear stuck her paw in front of the turtle's face.

"What do you think of fur, Turtle?" she asked, her fur rubbing the turtle's nose.

"It tickles," said the turtle, who suddenly sneezed.

The surprised bear jumped back.

Two eagles spread their wings. "Fur looks very heavy," said one eagle.

"Feathers are much better," said the other. "They're as soft as fur, as warm as fur, and they help us fly too."

The eagles flew down and fluttered over the turtle.

"Don't you agree, Turtle?" the eagles asked.

The turtle had never wanted to fly, but she wasn't going to disagree.

"Feathers are useful," said the turtle. "No doubt about it."

The eagles returned to their perch.

The porcupine shook herself. "Feathers are fine for birds, I guess," she said, "but they're no match for quills. Now quills come in handy. When I want to go somewhere, I never wait in line. Everybody gets out of my way."

She stuck her quills in front of the turtle.

"Would you get out of my way if I wanted?" she asked the turtle.

"Oh, yes," said the turtle. "I'd avoid you as much as possible."

The porcupine frowned. She was about to say something more when she felt a raindrop.

"Oh, no," she said.

The other animals looked up. "Did you feel that?" said the bear.

"It's starting to rain," said the lion. When the lion's mane got wet, it got snarled. He ran into a cave at once.

When the snakes' skin got wet, they slipped and slid all over the place. So they darted into a hole in the ground.

When the bear's fur got wet, dirt stuck to it, and she got muddy. She squeezed into a hollow tree.

When the eagles' feathers got wet, it was much harder to fly. They swooped under some tree branches.

When the porcupine's quills got wet, the water dripped off them for a long time. So she ran into the bushes.

The elephant just sighed. "There's nowhere big enough for me to hide," she said. "And the water somehow gets in my ears. I guess we all have to put up with the rain, though. Isn't that right, Turtle?"

The elephant looked down. The turtle said nothing, but the elephant could hear her chuckling inside her nice dry shell.

Think About It

1. Tell why the other animals picked on the turtle.
2. Why did the turtle have to think carefully before she answered each animal's question?
3. How does the old saying Those who laugh last, laugh best fit this story?
4. Which stories in this cluster teach a lesson? What lessons do they teach?

Create and Share

Pretend you have been asked by one of the animals to create a special rain covering. Draw a picture showing what you would make. Then write an ad you could use to sell it. Show other people your drawing and your ad.

Explore

Search for another book that tells how one animal's covering is special. When would this covering be a big help? When would it cause problems?

Spokes and Sprockets

Spokes and sprockets, pedals and brakes
Riding a bike is a piece of cake!

Michael Built a Bicycle

Michael built a bicycle
unsuitable for speed,
it's crammed with more accessories
than anyone could need,
there's an AM-FM radio,
a deck to play cassettes,
a refrigerator-freezer,
and a pair of TV sets.

There are shelves for shirts and sweaters,
there are hangers for his jeans,
a drawer for socks and underwear,
a rack for magazines,
there's a fishtank and a birdcage
perched upon the handlebars,
a bookcase, and a telescope
to watch the moon and stars.

There's a telephone, a blender,
and a stove to cook his meals,
there's a sink to do the dishes
somehow fastened to the wheels,
there's a portable piano,
and a set of model trains,
an automatic bumbershoot
that opens when it rains.

There's a desk for typing letters
on his fabulous machine,
a stall for taking showers,
and a broom to keep things clean,
but you'll never see him ride it,
for it isn't quite complete,
Michael left no room for pedals,
and there isn't any seat.

—*Jack Prelutsky*

The First True Bicycle

by Ruth Dana Pedersen

All his neighbors laughed at him. Even children gathered around the little cottage. They were hoping to get a glimpse at Mr. Kirkpatrick Macmillan. People tried to peek into the old shed he used as a workshop. They all thought something odd was going on in there.

Stories of Macmillan spread to Dumfries, the nearest town. Soon the townspeople, too, came to look and laugh. There were many wild tales told about the foolish country blacksmith. If he noticed the unkind laughs of his neighbors, he gave no sign. Kirkpatrick Macmillan had an idea for an invention and he kept working on it every spare minute.

This took place in Scotland in 1830. There had never been an invention quite like his. The inventor had to plan and then make all the parts by hand. It was slow work.

Sometimes, at dusk, his neighbors would catch a glimpse of it. The inventor would bring the contraption outside. He would push to start it, then jump on it and begin working furiously. What a rumbling and squeaking! What a dizzy ride! It seemed impossible to steer the thing as it bounced along, but the rider hung on. Sometimes it dumped him. How his neighbors laughed then!

His shop became a popular place. More people brought their horses to get shoes and their carts to be repaired. They all hoped to get a glimpse of the foolish invention. Later, whenever there was a gathering, they told tales about the inventor.

His family was so embarrassed and unhappy that they hated to go outside their cottage. The children didn't want to go to school.

Macmillan should have welcomed the new people coming to his shop. He needed the extra money. But he had less time for his invention. He was in such a hurry to finish it that he started getting up earlier in the mornings and working later at night. He rode his invention after dark.

The story spread that the machine had a wooden frame and large wheels made with wood and iron. No one knew what made it go. But many had seen it, with Macmillan riding it.

At last, one day in 1839, his invention was
complete. His family went to see the monster. It
had two wheels, a wide flat seat, and a gadget to
make it go. In front was a small horse's head
made of oak. None of his family was brave
enough to take a ride. This disappointed
Macmillan.

When he told them of his plans, his wife cried
and his children were fearful. He was going to
ride to the city of Glasgow, 70 miles away, to visit
his brothers.

The roads in those days were only stony, bumpy trails. Glasgow seemed a world away.

Macmillan started at dawn. He had to struggle furiously. It was a hard job. Sometimes he had to stop and rest. The invention bounced and clattered so loudly that people woke and looked out their windows. It was a cart without an animal to pull it.

Something went wrong. A wheel fell apart. He had to hire a boy to help him carry the parts home. His neighbors all laughed at his unhappy return.

His wife now hoped that he would forget about his invention. But Macmillan wasn't even discouraged. He was only sorry that his shop kept him so busy that he had little time for his invention.

He kept on trying. He made new parts. Then if they didn't work, he made changes. Months, then years went by before he finished his invention. It now had a brake.

One day in 1842, he thought he was ready to take that trip to Glasgow. This time he started at night. He wanted to avoid some of the people who would laugh at him.

Somehow the news spread. There was quite a gathering to see him off that night. He was happy when he left his shop to begin the long trip.

He sat on a hard, flat seat above two high wooden wheels. Ahead of him was the carved horse's head.

The contraption rattled and creaked as it bumped along. Its inventor worked furiously to keep it moving.

Some of the neighbors were surprised. Most thought it was a joke and its inventor was foolish. The children shouted, "Crazy Mack, get a horse!"

He rode on. It was a hard ride. In rocky parts the wheels wobbled and he had to get off and push the machine.

Things went well and the next day he was in Glasgow about noon.

Here in the city, many people crowded around. In his hurry to avoid these crowds, he ran into a child with his contraption. Although the child wasn't hurt, she cried loudly. So some angry men dragged the inventor before a judge.

During the questioning in court, Macmillan told the judge that he had come from Dumfries in two days.

The judge told Macmillan he shouldn't be riding a machine at 8 miles an hour in the city. He said it was dangerous to others. Then he fined Macmillan.

The judge and the men at court were curious to see the contraption. So the inventor showed them. He worked with all his might while he rode. The judge said it was a very clever machine. In fact, he was so pleased that he gave the fine back to Macmillan.

The inventor rode proudly home a few days later.

Macmillan never made any money from his invention. But other inventors, who had seen his machine, made his idea even better. They made faster, lighter machines. These became very popular.

Its inventor is buried beneath a stone dated 1879. It says that he was the inventor of the bicycle. But few of the people all over the world who ride bicycles have ever heard of Kirkpatrick Macmillan.

The inventor, even in his dreams, could never
have imagined the bicycle of today. Nor could he
have dreamed how popular his invention would
become.

Many persons helped with the invention of
what we now know as a bicycle. But Kirkpatrick
Macmillan was the one whose ideas and pedals
first made it go.

BICYCLES

Bicycles have certainly changed over the last 150 years since Kirkpatrick Macmillan's time. If he were to see one today, he might not even recognize his own invention.

People use bicycles for fun, as a sport, and for transportation. Imagine what bicyclists would do without Macmillan's pedals.

Think About It

1. In what ways were Michael and Macmillan alike?
2. What kind of problems did Macmillan have to face while inventing the bicycle?
3. Why do you think people made fun of Macmillan?
4. What reasons might explain why Macmillan refused to give up on what others thought was a crazy idea?
5. What is not practical about Michael's bicycle? About Macmillan's first bicycle?

Create and Share
Draw a picture of your dream bicycle. Label the parts and the special things you would put on it. Use your picture and describe your bicycle to someone else.

Explore
Look at the pictures in a bicycle catalog or magazine. Find some things that Michael or Macmillan might like to have put on their bicycles. Explain why you picked out each gadget.

GREG'S BIKE

from THAT JULIA REDFERN
by Eleanor Cameron

The heat was enough to make anyone dizzy.
Julia went weaving along the narrow path
through the vines. She got as far as the side
gate, and there was Greg's bike leaning against
the gatepost.

She stared at it with her usual huge desire. What she loved best in the world were Mama and Daddy and Uncle Hugh and Patchy-cat and sister—and Greg's bike. But she wasn't allowed to have a bike until she got older. Mama said she'd be too much of a danger on a bike of her own.

Greg was always supposed to put his bike away in the garage but this time he'd forgotten. He'd had something more important to do, and Julia knew what it was. She ran over to the fence and looked through. There were Greg and Bob, down on their knees in Bob's backyard sorting over old junk.

Julia turned and studied Greg's bike again. She'd pictured herself many times whizzing down hills. She could see herself jumping the bike over a curb into the street and leaping it up onto the sidewalk on the other side. It would be just as easy as anything, the way Greg always did. Then flashing around the playground at school and past her friend Maisie's house. Maisie would be out in front watching. Maisie's eyes would be big, and Julia would wave and disappear on down the street, leaving Maisie behind looking after her.

"Julia," said her father, "Aunt Alex and Uncle Hugh are going to drop by. So come on in now and get cleaned up." And he went off along the path and up the steps and into the house singing.

Julia frowned, furiously working things out. Then she went over to the bike and led it up the street to the top of the hill behind her house. Her heart was beating hard with excitement and fright. She could feel her chest shaking.

At the top of the hill she turned and looked
back down. There, on the other side of the
street, was a little flying figure, arms waving,
pigtails leaping out behind.

"You're gonna get it!" shouted Maisie.
"You're gonna get it—you just wait. Are you
ever gonna get it! *Greg's bike!*"

Julia let the bike crash and took off after
Maisie. "You mind your own business," she
yelled. "You be quiet and mind your own—" but
Maisie had already turned and run home again.
She bounced up her front steps, and had banged
the door behind her before Julia could so much as
get to Maisie's front walk. She stood there out of
breath. What if Greg had heard? Then she
turned and ran up to the top of the hill again.
Nothing could stop her now. *Nothing*, except if
Greg should come over the fence and out into the
street after her. But he was nowhere in sight.

She got the bike up again and tilted it so that she could fling a leg over and get onto the seat. Then she gave a push to get it started. It wobbled. Her feet searched for the pedals, but she couldn't reach. Away they went, slowly just for a second or two, then with horrible speed.

Julia was leaning forward, fingers gripping the handlebars. Her eyes were staring.

Her mouth was open. Her legs were stiff.

The hill was steep and made the bike go faster

—faster

—faster.

A car had pulled up alongside the curb and Uncle Hugh had gotten out. Then he went around to help Aunt Alex. He was standing with his back to Julia, as Aunt Alex looked up the hill. Her mouth opened but no cry would come. She pointed, waving her hands in terror. Julia was headed straight for them.

Uncle Hugh turned. Just as Julia was about to smash into them, he jerked Aunt Alex back at the very last second. Julia zinged past them and the bicycle scraped the telephone pole. She was hurled through the air and landed on the pavement on her back like a bug with her legs up. "Oh!" she gasped. "Oh! O-o-oh!" She was too stunned to cry. *Greg's ruined bike—his ruined, mashed-up bike! What would he say? What would he do to her?*

"That child—oh, that child! Hugh, she could have killed me. She could have injured me for life. And Greg's bicycle—!" cried Aunt Alex.

Julia opened her eyes and looked up at them. She made out the very large shape of Aunt Alex, a big white blur, and the dark, much slimmer shape of Uncle Hugh. Aunt Alex was standing, and there was a white hat on her head. Uncle Hugh was kneeling beside Julia. But now he and Aunt Alex seemed to float away, come back, and float off again.

"Uncle Hugh, I didn't mean—I didn't know—!"
"No," exclaimed Aunt Alex. "Of course not,
Julia Redfern. You never do mean or know. Get
up now."

Uncle Hugh helped her and she put her arms around his neck and gave him a hug. He gave her one back with a kiss on the cheek.

"Are you all in one piece?"

When they saw that no bones were broken, Uncle Hugh picked up Greg's bike. He gave it a thorough going-over.

"Scraped and bent!" stormed Aunt Alex. "Broken beyond repair, I haven't a doubt."

"Not at all, Alex," said Uncle Hugh. "It's perfectly all right." He wheeled it over to the fence and set it against the gatepost, just as Greg had left it. "Come now, Julia," he said, holding out his hand, "let's go in and not make a fuss— no harm done."

"But her parents should be told," said Aunt Alex. "That Julia almost killed me. There is no reason on earth why that child's parents—"

"Yes, yes, I know, Alex. I know. But we've come for a visit, to have fun—"

They went up onto the porch and inside. Julia tiptoed quickly away down the hall to her own room while the hellos and how-are-you's and just-fine's were being said. She stopped for a moment or two at her bedroom door, inside the room with just her head peeking out. She heard Daddy go into the kitchen, saying he was going to give them all fresh blackberries and cream and hot buttered muffins.

Aunt Alex said to Mama, "I think you should be told, without my making a scene, that I have just—"

"Oh, now, Alex!" said Uncle Hugh.

"—that I have just been almost run into and most horribly injured, and Greg's new bicycle almost ruined. Would you believe it, Julia took off from the top of the hill—the *top* of the hill, mind you, at her age—and came straight for me—"

"*On Greg's bike?*" said Julia's mother.

"On Greg's bike," answered Aunt Alex. "And it is my opinion that that child—"

Julia closed the door and sat down on her bed. She swallowed, and her heart began to beat the way it had when she was taking the bike out onto the sidewalk, knowing exactly what she was going to do. Then, hearing footsteps, she got up and was about to slip out the door that led into the garden. The hall door opened and there was Mama. She stood and looked at Julia. Julia looked at her.

Silence.

"You have been a very, very naughty girl. Aunt Alex is right. You could have hurt her terribly—and Uncle Hugh, too."

"Does Daddy—?" But the tears were bulging over and she couldn't finish.

"Of course he knows. Now get cleaned up and come out and sit quietly." And Mama closed the door and went away.

Think About It

1. Tell why Julia decided to ride the bike even though she probably knew she would get into trouble.
2. Why do you think Aunt Alex and Uncle Hugh had such different views about what happened?
3. If Julia had known what would happen, do you think she would have done what she did? Explain your answer.

Create and Share
Pretend you are Greg. Describe how you would feel and what you would say when you found out what had happened.

Explore
Eleanor Cameron has written several other books about Julia. You might want to read a chapter in one of these books. Beverly Cleary has also written about children who sometimes get into trouble. Read a chapter in one of her books and think about how Ramona, Henry Huggins, or Otis Spofford reminds you of Julia.

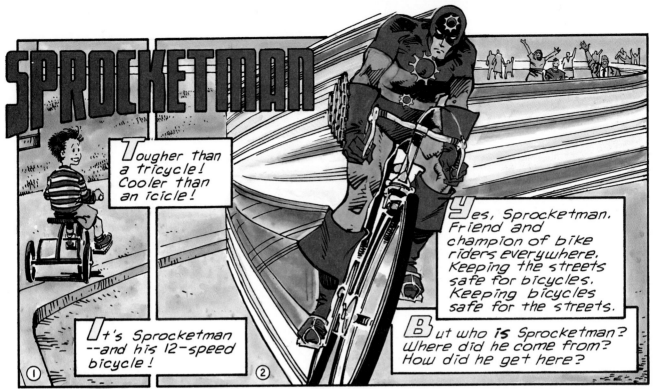

SPROCKETMAN

Tougher than a tricycle! Cooler than an icicle!

It's Sprocketman —and his 12-speed bicycle!

Yes, Sprocketman. Friend and champion of bike riders everywhere. Keeping the streets safe for bicycles. Keeping bicycles safe for the streets.

But who is Sprocketman? Where did he come from? How did he get here?

Let's just say it was a long and winding road...

To BEACH

Waves, here we come!

Come on, let's pass this guy.

Heads up!

KRESHH!

YOU TWERP!

VVWHEEOOOOOOOOO

EMERGENCY

16. Sorry, but I don't *have* time!

17. Don't ride on busy city sidewalks, fella!

18. And you! Aren't *you* going to lock your bike?

19. SCRRREEECH!

20. BWRANG!

Not again!

21. Nice catch!

So long, Mary. I straightened your wheel rim. Next time, I'd wear a helmet!

22.

23. How did he know my name?

'Bye, Sprocketman!

24. *Y*es, goodbye for now, Sprocketman. We'll all sleep a little better tonight knowing you're around to help keep the streets safe for bike riders and bike riders safe for the streets!

190

BICYCLE RULES OF THE ROAD

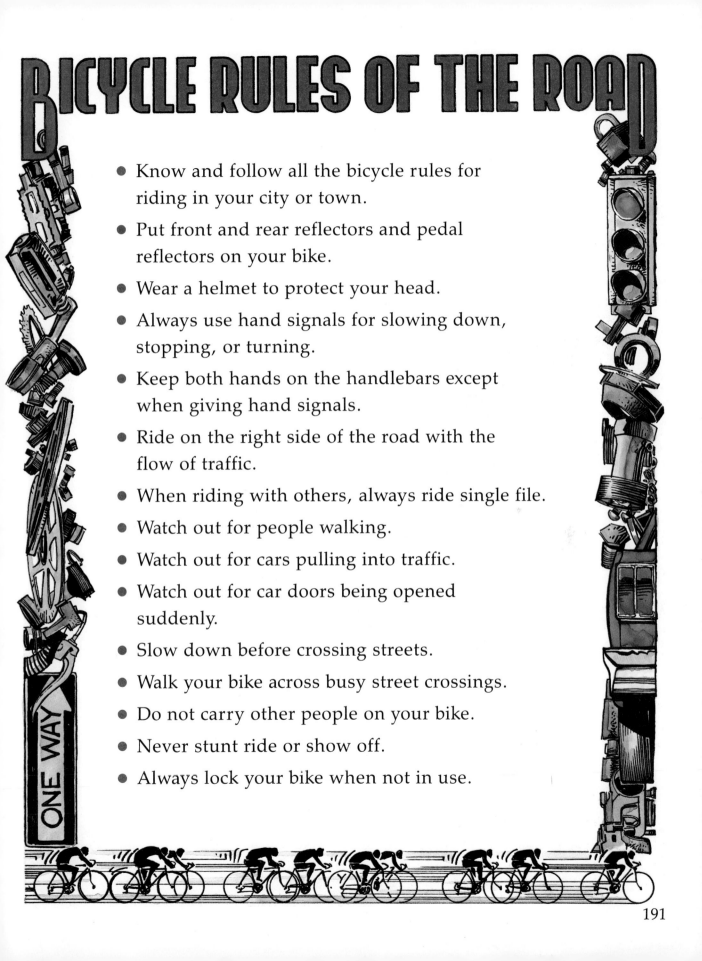

- Know and follow all the bicycle rules for riding in your city or town.
- Put front and rear reflectors and pedal reflectors on your bike.
- Wear a helmet to protect your head.
- Always use hand signals for slowing down, stopping, or turning.
- Keep both hands on the handlebars except when giving hand signals.
- Ride on the right side of the road with the flow of traffic.
- When riding with others, always ride single file.
- Watch out for people walking.
- Watch out for cars pulling into traffic.
- Watch out for car doors being opened suddenly.
- Slow down before crossing streets.
- Walk your bike across busy street crossings.
- Do not carry other people on your bike.
- Never stunt ride or show off.
- Always lock your bike when not in use.

ONE WAY

DIAGRAM OF A BICYCLE

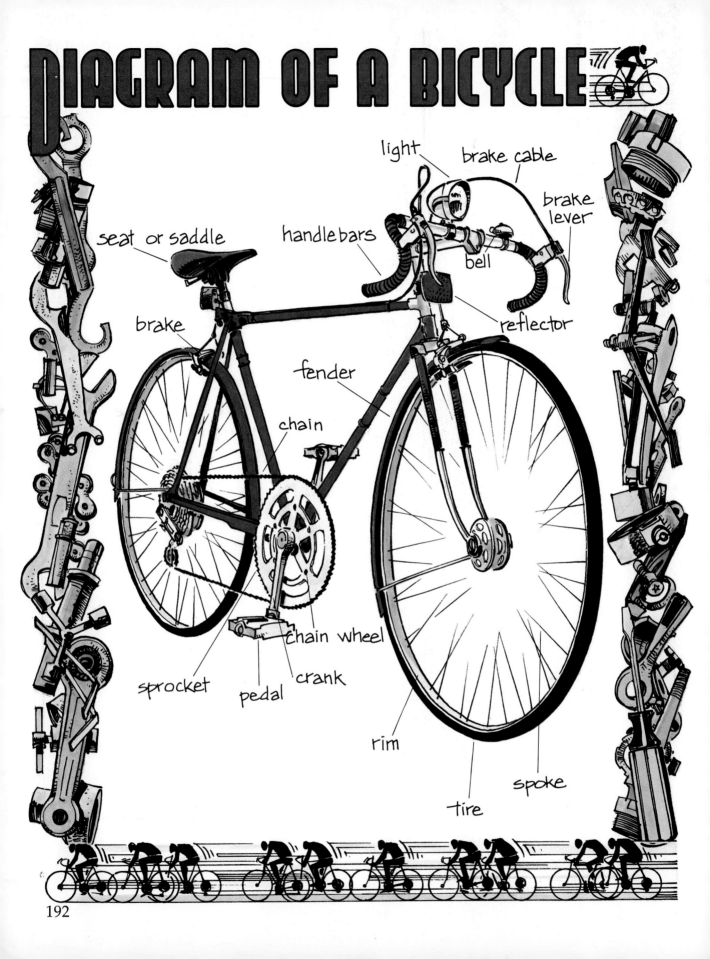

light

brake cable

brake lever

seat or saddle

handlebars

bell

brake

reflector

fender

chain

chain wheel

sprocket

crank

pedal

rim

spoke

tire

Think About It

1. Why did Sprocketman become involved in bicycle safety?
2. Why is Sprocketman a good character to teach bicycle safety?
3. Tell how Sprocketman could help in the place where you live.
4. Why is bicycle care an important part of bicycle safety?
5. Imagine that Sprocketman could talk to Julia Redfern and Michael. What advice would he give to them? What questions might they ask him?

Create and Share
Think about when you learned to ride a bike. Draw a comic strip showing what happened. In it, show someone teaching you something about bicycle safety.

Explore
Ask a parent or another adult about the rules of the road for cars. Find out about the test these adults had to pass and how they studied for it.

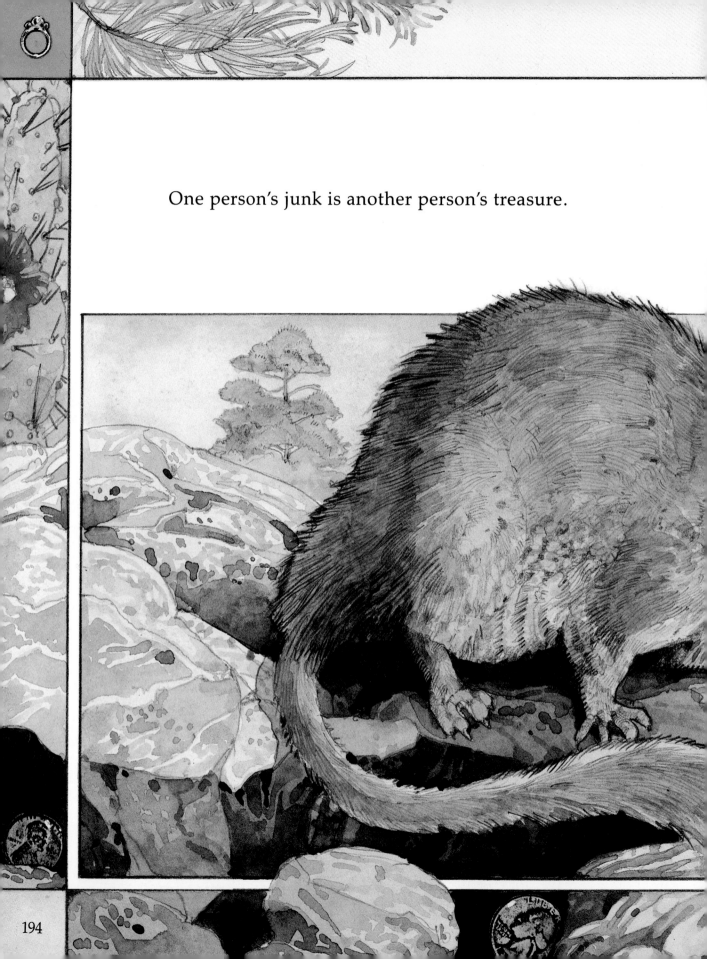

One person's junk is another person's treasure.

Hidden Treasures

Me and Goat McGee

by Betsy Byars

Last Saturday my friend Goat McGee and I hid
treasures for each other to find. Mine was
seventeen pennies, a knife with two blades, a
decal, and a balloon, all stuffed into a metal
Band-Aid box. I buried it in a pot of geraniums
on my front porch.

Then I made a map that was very clever. It
would lead Goat all over the neighborhood. And
not only was it clever, it looked like a real pirate
map. I had drawn it on brown paper and burned
the edges. I was proud of that map.

After I finished, I walked to the corner where
Goat and I had planned to meet. Goat had
probably been busy hiding a treasure for me and
making a map, and he looked pleased with
himself, too. He was standing there with a big
smile on his face.

I handed him my map. He handed me a scrap
of paper.

197

"What's this?" I asked.

"Clues."

"Clues? You were supposed to draw a map."
I looked at the piece of paper. It was so little, it
was hard to read. Finally I made it out:

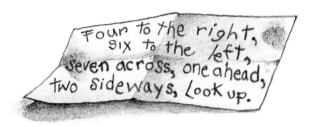

"What's this, Goat?" I asked again, but Goat
was already running down the sidewalk. It
looked to me as if he were heading straight for
my house and the pot of geraniums.

Four to the right. Quickly I took four steps to
the right. *Six to the left.* I did that. *Seven across,
one ahead, two sideways.* I ended up standing in
almost the same place. I looked up. All I could
see were some clouds in the sky.

"Goat!" I ran after him. When I got to my
house, he was standing on the porch. He had
already pulled my mom's geranium right out of
the pot, spilling the dirt all over. The Band-Aid
box was in his hand.

"Found it!" he said.

"Goat, you didn't even look at my map! I
spent all morning on that map!"

"I didn't need to," Goat said. "I saw a piece of geranium caught on your watch—look, right there. Then I knew—you hid it in the old geranium pot."

"That's not fair." I felt cheated. "You were supposed to use the map."

"I would have if I had needed it. Did you find your treasure yet?" He knew that I hadn't.

"No."

"Too tricky, huh?" Goat said.

"I haven't even had a chance to read the clues." I glanced down at the piece of paper, trying to look like I was reading it for the first time. "It's not so tricky."

Goat said, "It's trickier than yours," and he stuck my mom's geranium carelessly back into the pot. He opened the Band-Aid box and shook out the contents. Then he said, "Money—I can use that." He put it in his pocket. "A broken knife—"

"It's not broken."

"It's only got two blades."

"Well, it still cuts."

"A decal that came out of a cereal box—I know because I eat the same kind. And a balloon that says—let's see—*I was a good patient.* I know where you got that, from our dentist. He stopped giving them to me, because I bit him." Goat looked at me. "Well, go ahead. Find your treasure."

I stared back at him. All week I had been
looking forward to hiding treasures. Now he had
ruined it. And not only that, but for the first
time I knew how he got his nickname. He really
looked like a goat.

I opened the front door. "I'm bored with this."

"So, it's too tough for you, huh? Go ahead
and quit."

"I'm not quitting."

"Then find the treasure. I want to see if you
can do it."

"All right!" I stamped down the steps, down
the sidewalk. Goat followed. I could hear him
flipping the top of the metal box open, snapping
it shut.

"You have to start at the corner," he called.

"I know where to start."

"I just wanted to be helpful, pal."

We walked to the corner without saying anything else. I kept looking at the scrap of paper. I had held it so long that the writing was getting smeared. *Four to the right.*

Four what? I knew it was not steps. I had already tried that. Maybe it was giant steps. Maybe it was minutes. Walk four minutes to the right? With Goat McGee, it could mean anything.

When we got to the corner, I was still looking at the scrap of paper. Four blocks maybe. No, that would put us on the other side of the superhighway. And no one's allowed to walk across.

"I'll give you one more clue," Goat said. "It's not four blocks. That would put us across—"

"I know!"

"Then what do you think it is?" he asked.

"Houses maybe? Four houses?" I looked down the street.

"How could it be houses?" Goat said. "You can go four houses to the right, but how can you go six houses to the left? There aren't any houses back there."

"No, nothing but trees," I mumbled.

Goat McGee stuck his hands in his pockets. It was a quick movement and it gave him away as surely as the piece of geranium had given me away. I began to feel much better.

"Let's see, now," I said, starting down the sidewalk. "Could it be four *trees*? One—two—three—four trees?"

Goat followed. "That's not fair. I gave it away."

"Six trees to the left. Now, what's the next clue? *Seven across.* It has to be across that way. Yes, there are seven trees."

Goat was following me more slowly. "You didn't really figure it out. I gave it away."

"Well, so did I. You didn't even have to look at my map. All right, *one ahead, two sideways, look up.* Aha!"

There was a small paper bag hanging from the limb overhead. I took it down and opened it. Inside was half a package of breath mints, a Matchbox car with one wheel missing, and two bird feathers.

"How do you like your treasure?" Goat asked finally.

"Everything I always wanted."

"Look, if you don't want the breath mints, I'll put them back in my mom's purse."

"I want them. And if you don't want the knife, you can give that back to me."

"I want it."

I put all the stuff in my pocket, and Goat and I stood there for a moment. Goat looked down at his shoes and then over at me. "Want to do it again?" he asked. "Treasure hunt?"

"I guess."

"Maps or clues?"

"I'll do a map—you do clues."

"Fine with me," Goat said, "only I'm not going to give it away this time."

"Me either."

"Let's get going."

And we ran in opposite directions for home.

Think About It

1. Why was the storyteller upset with Goat McGee?
2. Were Goat's clues clever? Tell why or why not.
3. Which of these treasures would you have wanted to find?
4. Which part of the game do you think each character liked best?
5. Do you think either of these boys would make a good detective? Explain your answer.

Create and Share   Pick an object in your classroom. Draw a map or make up clues leading someone to that object. Share your map or clues with a classmate to see if he or she can guess what object you picked.

Explore   Find another story or a book that tells about games.

Where Is Beale's Treasure?

by Hal Ober

Here is a mystery that no one has ever solved. Like all the best mysteries, it's a true story.

In the state of Virginia—somewhere up in the mountains near Goose Creek—there is a buried treasure. People have been looking for this treasure for over one hundred years. No one knows exactly where it is. There is no treasure map to point the way. There is only one clue: a message written in a secret code. So far no one has been able to figure out the code. Maybe one day someone will. It could be you.

The story of Beale's treasure began in the year 1817. America was a young country then. The land was wild and full of adventure. So was a young man named Thomas Jefferson Beale. Beale lived in Virginia, and liked to go exploring. In 1817 he went out west with a group of other men. They were hoping to find buffalo and maybe a few grizzly bears. They did better than that. North of Santa Fe, New Mexico, they found gold.

In fact they found more than gold. After Beale's group began to dig a mine, they found silver. Soon they had so much silver and gold that it became a problem. Where could they keep all this treasure? Where would it be safe?

Today, of course, we put our treasure in a bank. In Thomas Beale's time many people believed that their own secret hiding places were safer than banks.

So, in 1819 Beale came back to Virginia. He rode up into Bedford County and crossed Goose Creek. Somewhere in the mountains, in a secret spot, he buried his treasure of silver and gold. Two years later he returned with more treasure for his secret hiding place.

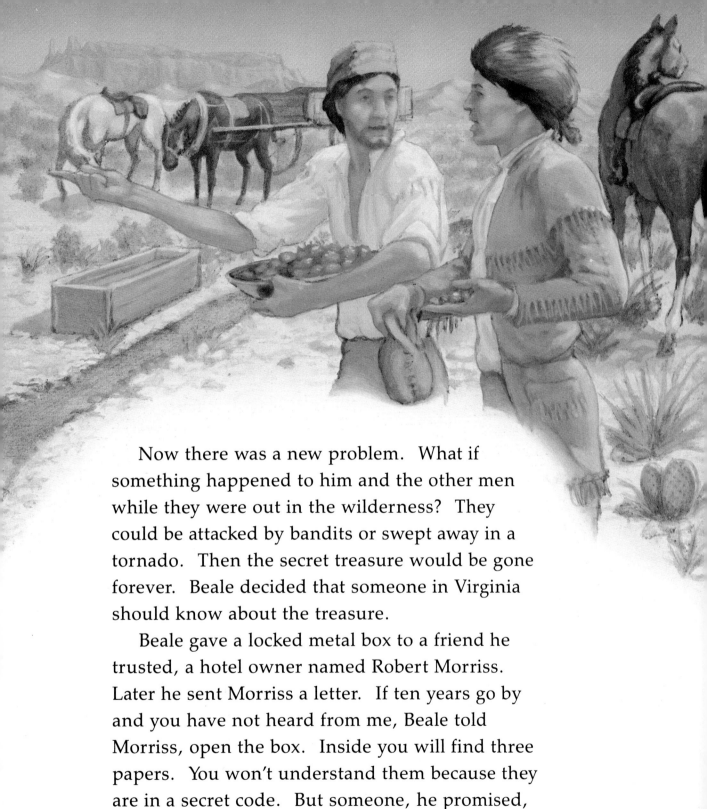

Now there was a new problem. What if
something happened to him and the other men
while they were out in the wilderness? They
could be attacked by bandits or swept away in a
tornado. Then the secret treasure would be gone
forever. Beale decided that someone in Virginia
should know about the treasure.

Beale gave a locked metal box to a friend he
trusted, a hotel owner named Robert Morriss.
Later he sent Morriss a letter. If ten years go by
and you have not heard from me, Beale told
Morriss, open the box. Inside you will find three
papers. You won't understand them because they
are in a secret code. But someone, he promised,
will send you a key to figure out the codes.

Morriss never saw or heard from Beale again. He gave Beale much longer than ten years. He waited over twenty years before he opened the box. There were three mysterious papers. Each one had a long list of numbers. There was also another letter from Beale. It explained that the first list of numbers told *where* the treasure was buried. The second list told *what* the treasure was. The third list told *who* was to get the treasure. The key was supposed to help figure out what the numbers meant.

No one ever sent Morriss the key to the codes. He tried to figure out what the numbers meant for many years. Finally he gave up. One year before his death he gave all the papers to a friend named James Ward. Ward worked with the numbers too. In fact, for the next thirty years he did very little else. Luckily some of the hard work paid off. He was able to crack Code Number Two! Thanks to Ward we know that the treasure is over four tons of gold and silver, worth many millions of dollars!

How did he do it? Ward discovered that the key to Code Number Two is the Declaration of Independence. It turned out that each number in the code secretly stood for the *first letter* of every word in the Declaration. When he put all those first letters together, there was the message.

It would have been nice if the Declaration of Independence had worked for the other two codes, but it didn't. Ward tried it backwards and forwards. Then he gave up too.

Will anyone ever crack the code and discover the secret hiding place of Beale's treasure? Maybe. Anyone can try. You can ask for a copy of the three secret codes by writing to the Roanoke Public Library in Roanoke, Virginia.

Meanwhile, why not read some books about codes and practice some codes of your own. Anything can stand for a letter—a number, a color, a shape, or another letter. If you can read this message, you're on your way to cracking other codes. Use every other letter in these five letter "words." Put them together and see if you can figure out the message.

AGROP OWDYL MUNCH KLARN IDAHO ALVIE PFLUG NYORK? Okay!

Think About It

1. What things did Beale do to make sure his treasure would be safe?
2. What do you think happened to the key that Morriss was supposed to get?
3. Do you think anyone will ever be able to find Beale's treasure? Why or why not?
4. Why do you think people are so interested in buried treasure and secret codes?

Create and Share
Pretend you have cracked Beale's code and found the treasure. List some of the things you would do with the money. Then pick the three most important things and write a paragraph telling why you listed them.

Explore
Find out more about the Declaration of Independence. Who wrote it? When was it written? Why was it written? What link is there between Beale's name and that of the writer of the Declaration of Independence?

The Shepherd's Treasure

a Persian folktale
retold by Mark Morano

Once upon a time there was a poor man who herded sheep in Persia. He lived by himself in a cave. The only thing he owned was a sheepskin. He wore the sheepskin over his tattered clothes during the day. At night he would pull the sheepskin around him to keep warm. The old sheepskin was his best friend.

Over the years, as the shepherd took care of his sheep, he learned many things. He listened to the birds, and their songs taught him the joy of life. He watched the sky and clouds and learned when the rain would fall. He also learned about people. He made friends with other shepherds and listened to their problems. They told their friends about the wise shepherd and how he had helped them. Many people went to the shepherd for help. Little by little, everyone heard about the wise shepherd. Soon even the Shah heard of the shepherd and how he helped anyone who came to him.

The Shah was a good king and was always looking for wise people to help rule his country. When he heard about the shepherd, the Shah decided to see how wise he was. He told his servant he would disguise himself as a poor traveler. First he gave his servant all his good clothes. Next he put on the oldest clothes he could find.

The Shah took some fruit and nuts, and rode off on a donkey to find the shepherd. After a long ride he found the shepherd herding his sheep. The Shah started talking to the shepherd and asked him to share his food. While they ate, the Shah asked the shepherd many questions.

The Shah then said, "Thank you for sharing lunch, but I must leave. I am a poor traveler who has a long way to go."

The shepherd smiled. "It is all right. I know it is a long ride back to the palace."

The Shah was surprised that the shepherd knew he was the king. He sat and thought for a moment. "Even though I was disguised as a poor traveler, you knew I was the king. How is that?"

The shepherd answered, "Shah, even though your clothes are tattered, you wear them like a king. You speak as if you are used to people obeying. It is easy to see you are not a poor traveler."

"I now know that you are a wise man as everyone has told me," said the Shah. "Because you are so wise, I will make you the governor of this part of my country."

At first everyone was happy that the shepherd was the new governor because they loved and trusted him. But before long, people noticed that the governor always had with him a camel carrying a heavy chest with two locks. The people began to talk to each other about what was in the chest.

"Why does he have two locks?" someone asked. "Do you think there is treasure inside?"

"Maybe he keeps the gold we pay for taxes in that chest," said a friend.

"That isn't right. That gold is for the Shah. Does our new governor keep it for himself?" wondered another.

Soon the Shah heard stories that the people were not happy with their new governor. He was angry when he found out that everyone said the new governor was stealing his gold.

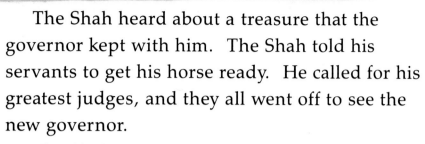

The Shah heard about a treasure that the governor kept with him. The Shah told his servants to get his horse ready. He called for his greatest judges, and they all went off to see the new governor.

The Shah rode up to the governor and said, "What are these stories I have heard about you stealing my gold? And what is this treasure of yours?"

The governor shook his head. "I haven't taken any of your gold," he said.

"If you haven't," said the angry Shah, "then open your treasure chest and show me what is inside."

The governor had his servants take the heavy chest down from the camel's back. He took two keys from his pocket and opened the two locks.

The Shah and his judges leaned forward. The governor opened the chest and took out the treasure inside. It was his old sheepskin. He held it up so everyone could see and said, "When I was a poor shepherd this was my best friend. It covered me each day and warmed me at night. I have kept it safe in this chest so that I would never forget that I was once poor. It helps me remember that even though I am rich, I am no better than anyone else."

The Shah smiled and said, "This man is indeed a wise and good governor. From this day on, he will be the greatest of all my governors."

And so the governor who was once a poor shepherd became one of the most important men in Persia. But he always kept his treasure, the old sheepskin, which had been his best friend.

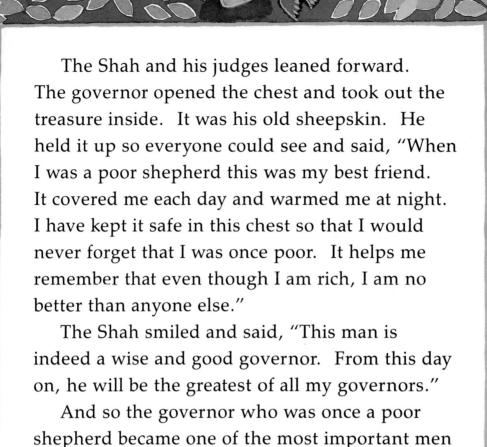

Think About It

1. What kind of man was the shepherd? Find places in the story that describe him.
2. Tell why the Shah made a good choice when he made the shepherd a governor.
3. How did the people probably feel when they saw the shepherd's treasure? Why did they feel this way?
4. In what ways does the saying Things are not always what they seem to be fit this story?
5. How did this story help you to start thinking about treasures in a new way?

Create and Share   Pretend you work for a newspaper. You are there when the shepherd opens the chest. Write a news story about what happens. Remember to tell who, what, where, why, and when in your story.

Explore   What book or story would you put in a treasure chest? Why?

HERBERT'S TREASURE

by Alice Low

Herbert was a treasure collector. He liked everything about collecting treasures.

He liked getting up in the morning and thinking about what he would find that day. He liked leaving his house and going to the old town dump. He liked searching in the big pile of junk near the collapsed old barn, finding treasures, bringing them home, and arranging them in his room.

He liked looking at them, too. Everywhere he looked in his room there was some kind of treasure—hinges, a hammer, a mirror, some wire, pieces of glass, and a bicycle tire. He just liked having treasures.

His mother didn't like it though. It was very hard to clean his room. Every week, day after day, she said, "Herbert, please, Herbert, throw something away!"

"I can't," Herbert said. "They're treasures."

"Junk!" said his mother. "Nothing but junk!"

"You never know," Herbert said. "They might come in handy—someday."

"This rusty can?" his mother said.

"I can keep things in it," Herbert said. He picked up three screws, four nails, and a doorbell and put them in the can.

When his mother left, he dumped them out to look at them. The doorbell didn't work, but it might—someday. Most of all, he liked thinking about his treasures and what he could do with them—someday. And so every afternoon—in rain or sun—when other boys were playing baseball or going to the movies, Herbert went to the dump. He went by himself, so he wouldn't have to share his treasures. He found a rusty saw, a clock with no hands, a screwdriver, bricks, and some paint pots and pans and carried them home.

Herbert's mother said, "Why do you go to that messy dump when our yard is so neat and nice and we have croquet and a swing and everything just right for *you?*"

"It's more fun in the dump," Herbert said.

"Get rid of that junk, Herbert, right now, today. Herbert, please, Herbert, throw *something* away!"

"Okay," Herbert said. "Tomorrow."

The next day he brought back a broken shovel, some chair rungs from chairs, bedposts and table legs, stair treads from stairs. And a real find—a lock. He put them on top of his toys on the shelves.

"Now look at your toys!" his mother said. "All squashed under that junk. I *mean* it, Herbert, right now, today. *Please*, Herbert, *please*, throw something away."

"All right," Herbert said. He took everything off his shelves and made two piles—one to keep and one to throw away.

Then he threw away the throwaway pile. After he'd arranged his treasures on his toy shelves, he thought about the lock. It didn't work, but it might—someday.

Every day he brought home more—window panes, picture frames, planks from old floors, shingles and doorknobs and frames from old doors. The mountain in the dump got smaller and smaller.

Herbert's room got more and more crowded.
He had to make a path through the treasures to
get to his bed. And it was very hard to open the
door.

It was exciting to look around his room, but it
was sad to go to the dump now because there was
almost nothing left to find. The only treasure left
was an old carved door.

He dragged it home on his wagon—slowly.
He needed time to figure out where to put it. By
the time he got to his room he knew.

First he had to sweep out the treasures from
under his bed. There was only one place to put
them—on top of his bed. Finally, he slid the door
under his bed. That night he slept on the floor.

The next morning his mother was furious.
She said, "This is the limit. I mean it. Today!
Herbert, please, Herbert, throw something
away!"

"Don't worry, there's nothing more to find,"
said Herbert sadly. "Unless—maybe—there's
something *under*ground."

Herbert set out with his shovel and began to dig. Digging was harder, but more fun, too, because you never knew what might be under there.

Mostly there were rocks. Then one day his shovel struck something hard that went *clang!* Metal! Only metal rang that way.

He dug it up, scratched off the dirt, and washed it with the hose until he could see what it was. A key!

It didn't fit the car door, or the kitchen door, or the front door. But it had to open something somewhere. Nobody would make a key that didn't open anything.

He polished it, put it under his pillow, and thought about it every night. It might be the key to a chest full of gold pieces. Then he could buy anything he wanted. He'd like that. Except where would he put all the new things?

Maybe it was the key to a castle dungeon. He would rescue the princess imprisoned there. Then he'd be a hero.

Or maybe—this was even better—a key to the *whole* castle where he'd be the king. Not a castle full of gold thrones and red carpets; an empty castle with nothing in it—except his treasures. And nobody else would live there. It would be his own castle where no one could say, "Herbert, please, Herbert, throw something away!"

He could see it in his dream. He could see himself coming in the door with more and more treasures. The door was old and carved and nobody else could open it because *he* had the key. He could see the lock, too, rusty and old.

He woke up. The moon was shining on the rusty lock. He took the key from under his pillow, and slowly, his heart thumping, tried the key in the lock. It didn't fit. Not quite. He oiled the lock and tried the key again. This time it fit! He turned it slowly. CLICK! The lock opened. The key fit the lock!

And the lock fit the door! He screwed it in
and screwed on the doorknob—and then he went
to sleep.

In the morning he woke up and saw the door
with the key in the lock. Then he remembered.
It was going to be a busy day. He had a plan.

First he dragged everything outdoors. His
mother didn't ask what he was doing. She was
just glad he was doing it—outdoors.

He sawed and hammered for three days until
he was almost finished. Then he set in the
doorframe and hinged on the door. And finally,
he opened the door with his key and moved
everything in.

Then Herbert hammered some more, and painted some too. There were plenty of shelves—shelves for his paint pots and clock with no hands, his tire and his wire and his tools and his pans. And for everything else.

Last of all, he moved himself in. It *was* a castle, just like the one in his dream. The floorboards were warped, and the windows were cracked, but there was plenty of room—room for his treasures and no one to say, "Herbert, please, Herbert, throw something away!"

The doorbell still doesn't work, but it might—someday.

Think About It

1. Why did Herbert think the things he found at the dump were treasures?
2. Why was Herbert's mother so upset with him?
3. How did Herbert come up with a solution to the problem of so many treasures?
4. How do you think Herbert's mother felt when she saw what he had done with his treasures?
5. All of the stories in HIDDEN TREASURES deal with different kinds of treasure. Which kind of treasure do you think is most important? Why?

Create and Share

Think up a special place to keep your own treasures. Draw a picture of what your treasure place looks like. Describe some of the treasures.

Explore

Find a book about other hidden treasure. You might want to look for stories about pirate treasure or deep-sea treasure.

Blast Off!

Firefly, airplane, satellite, star—
How I wonder which you are.

by William Cole

THE PLANET PARADE

by Jane Foster Thornton

Characters

Mercury		Jupiter
Venus	Sun	Saturn
Earth		Uranus
Mars		Pluto
Neptune		

Setting: *A bare stage*

At Rise: **Mercury, Venus, Earth, Mars, Jupiter, Saturn, Uranus, Neptune,** *and* **Pluto** *are lined up at rear of stage, backs to audience. Each holds a ball that shows the size of the planet he or she stands for.* **Sun,** *bouncing huge yellow ball, enters right.*

Sun: Hello! Hello! I am the Sun!
Today we'll have a lot of fun!
But first, here is my family—
Nine planets, as you all can see.

(**Planets** *turn around, come toward the audience and line up behind Sun. They sing "You Are My Sunshine." When they finish,* **Sun** *bows to them.*)

Thank you all. I love you, too.
But now we have some work to do.
Take your places, one by one,
Orbiting around the Sun.

Mercury: I'm the closest. Look at me!
I am little Mercury.

(Starts circling around Sun)

Venus: I am Venus. I'm not far.
I'm sometimes called the Evening Star.

(Circles around Mercury and Sun)

Earth: My name is Earth. I'm blue and
green,
With hills and mountains in between.

(Circles around other planets and Sun)

Mars: Make way for Mars! I'm fourth in line.
Round and round—I'm doing fine.

(Circles)

Jupiter: Here comes Jupiter. Look, you all!
I'm so big and you're so small.

(Circles)

Saturn: Next comes Saturn. See my rings?
They're really quite amazing things.

(Circles)

Uranus: I'm Uranus. I spin on my side.
I'm much too big to try to hide.

(Circles)

Neptune: Neptune's next. I'm cold as ice,
But way out here in space, it's nice!

(Circles)

Pluto: I am Pluto. Though I'm small,
I'm the farthest out of all.

(Circles)

Sun: Good for you! You're doing fine.
But now, here's an idea of mine.

(**Planets** *stop circling to listen.*)

I'll decide who is the best,
The planet who outshines the rest.

(**Planets** *huddle together left.* **Venus** *steps out.*)

Venus: I'm the brightest one above,
Named for Venus, Queen of Love.
I dazzle everybody's eyes.
Surely I should win the prize!

(**Mercury** *pushes Venus away.*)

Mercury: I'm not the youngest or the oldest,
Nor the smallest, hottest, coldest,
But I'm fastest. Can't you see
You should give the prize to me?

(**Uranus** *elbows Mercury out of the way.*)

Uranus: I'm the seventh from the sun.
I've many moons, not just one.
I used to be King George's Star.
I'm much better than you are!

(**Jupiter** *pulls Uranus away.*)

Jupiter: I'm so big that all you there
Could fit inside with room to spare!

(**Mars** *takes Jupiter's place.*)

Mars: It isn't only moons or size
That settles who should win the prize.
Mysterious Mars, whose glow is red
Should surely be the one instead!

(**Neptune** *pushes Mars aside.*)

Neptune: My year has sixty thousand days.
I cannot feel the Sun's warm rays.
I'm so cold I'm turning blue,
So I should win the prize, not you!

(**Pluto** *edges out Neptune.*)

Pluto: You think *you're* cold—why,
   you're no hero!
I'm four hundred degrees below zero!
And since I'm farthest from the Sun,
I think that I should be the one.

Sun: You all are special, that is true.
But Earth, we haven't heard from you.

Earth: There really isn't much to say.
Day follows night, night follows day.
I'm not too new, I'm not too old,
I'm not too hot, I'm not too cold.
I have one moon, not two or three,
But one is quite enough for me.

Sun: Can't you tell us something more,
That we haven't heard before?

Earth: I have trees, and grass, and sky,
Animals, and birds that fly,
Flowers growing in the ground,
And people—people all around!

All: People? People, did you say?
People? People? What are they?

Earth: Earthlings you would say
Live and grow and work and play.
They climb my trees and breathe my
air.
They live here and here and there.

(**Earth** *points to different parts of him/
herself.*)

We work together—big and small
To make our world the best of all.

Sun: All my planet family
Are very, very dear to me.
But I will give the prize this minute
To Earth and all the people in it!

(**Sun** *hangs large golden sun-shaped medal around neck of Earth and* **planets** *clap for Earth.*)

Now back to work—around you go.
Mercury, Venus, don't be slow.

(*As* **Sun** *calls their names, planets go back to rotating around Sun.*)

Earth, Mars, Jupiter, Saturn too,
  Uranus and Neptune follow you.
Last comes Pluto from afar—
All circle round the Sun, your star!

(**Planets** *go back to orbiting around Sun, and skip around, singing "You Are My Sunshine."*)

Think About It

1. Share some new facts about planets that you learned from reading the play.
2. Tell why Earth won Sun's prize.
3. Why was Sun the big boss in the play?
4. Which other planet would you like to visit? Why?
5. Would you have given Sun's prize to a different planet? Why or why not?

Create and Share   Write a poem that tells what Sun might say if the planets decided to give it a prize.

Explore   Pick a planet. Do some more reading about that planet. Write a paragraph describing why you think your planet deserves Sun's prize.

BLAST OFF!

by William Teal

Imagine that you are a crew member on a space flight. You are zooming through space at thousands of miles an hour. Suddenly, the cockpit computer screen flashes—DANGER! A damaged box in the cargo bay is giving off dangerous gases. Should you end the mission and return to Earth? Or should you see if the damage must first be fixed? To find out, you have to take a space walk. Your heart is racing as you put on your space suit and step out of the cabin. But you are not in space at all.

You're at U.S. SPACE CAMP, in Huntsville, Alabama. It's at the world's largest space museum, The Space and Rocket Center. You're taking part in a training course. It's for kids who want to know what it's like to travel in space.

Kids come from all over the United States for the five-day spring and summer course. They have a special interest in space.

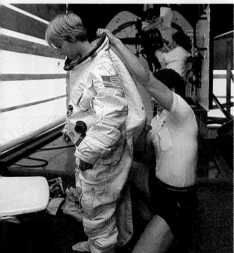

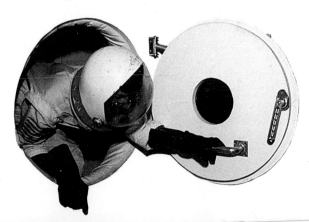

At the camp, kids climb aboard and train on equipment that was once used by NASA astronauts. Most of the equipment shows the campers the same kind of action that would happen in space. One machine is like a space capsule. Another teaches astronauts how to walk on the moon. By using this equipment, astronauts learn what it will be like up in space.

At the space center, campers start with some basic training. Day one is *Rocketry Day.* Campers do the same kind of morning exercises that the astronauts do. Then campers divide into groups. There are twelve members on each team. Now they are ready to work with the camp computer.

Without computers, space flight would be impossible. Some of the math problems that need to be solved to get off the ground would take weeks to finish with only pencil and paper. Campers soon learn to use the computer to figure out how to build model rockets. Of course, the model rockets don't have nearly as much power as space rockets. But they work the same basic way.

On day two, *Astronaut Training Day,* the kids get a taste of what it's like to live in space. They taste the same freeze-dried food the astronauts eat. Kids planning to go to the moon will have to know more than how to add water to freeze-dried food. They'll have to learn how to walk on the moon. Campers try out the moon walk training chair. They feel like they are walking on the moon, where they would weigh much less than they do on Earth.

Life in space can be dangerous. To deal with the lack of air, for example, astronauts use a space suit. Campers try on suits like those worn by the astronauts who landed on the moon in 1969. The space suit had 21 layers. It did a great job of protecting the astronauts from the hot and cold in space. Today's space suits are much lighter but they protect just as well.

On day three, *Micro Gravity Day,* campers get the chance to feel what it's like to work in weightlessness. The action takes place in a space walk training machine. The seat is a frame that floats above the floor on air. Equipment like this was used by astronauts to train for space walks! When a camper is in the seat, she can twist and turn in almost any direction, just like an astronaut who is weightless in space!

Later that day, the kids take out their swim suits. It's time to train for an emergency splashdown at sea. In a pool they try to climb from the water into a rubber raft without turning it over. From the raft they climb into a cage hanging over the pool. The cage feels as if it were hanging from a rescue helicopter at sea. The exercise isn't easy, even in shallow water. For astronauts, it would be more difficult during a real emergency in the ocean.

To give the astronauts a hand, there are robots. These robot helpers make it easier for the space crew to do their work. On day four, *Technology Day*, campers learn how to use the same kind of robot.

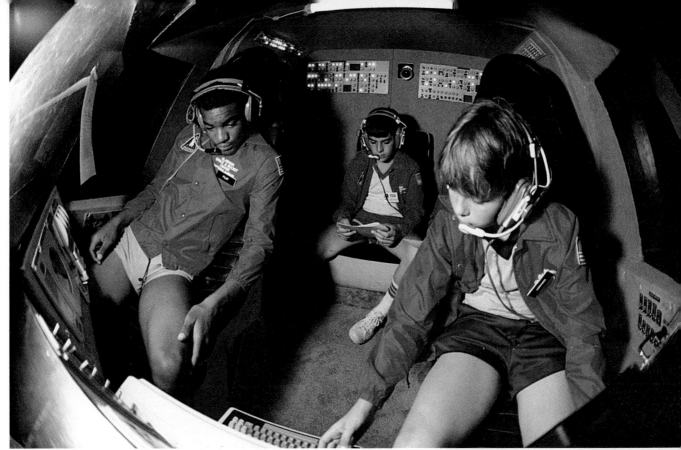

When the campers finish their basic training, they're ready for day five, *Mission Day.* It's time for the campers to launch their own space flight. The twelve members of each team work hard to finish this final test at SPACE CAMP.

Six members of each team act as mission control. These are the people who guide the flight from the ground. Six campers are given positions in the make-believe cockpit. Each camper has a job to do. On a real flight team, some astronauts are pilots and some are scientists with their own experiments to do.

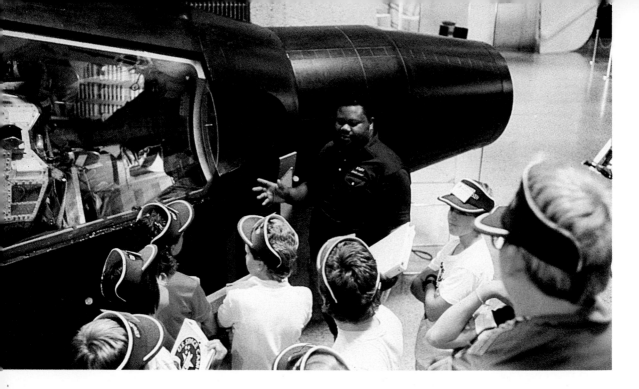

Shortly after lift-off, the computer signals that a box in the cargo bay is damaged. Campers must walk in space to solve the problem. After they do, the mission is over.

Finally, the crew comes down to Earth. They gather to talk about the flight. When it's all over, the kids each get a pair of SPACE CAMP wings that they proudly pin on their shirts.

For some of the campers, their week at SPACE CAMP could be just the beginning. Maybe one day they will live on the moon. Or maybe they'll live in huge space stations orbiting Earth. But whether they ever live in space or not, their week at SPACE CAMP was out of this world!

Think About It

1. What is the purpose of U.S. SPACE CAMP?
2. In what ways is the spaceflight on *Mission Day* like a real flight? In what ways is it make-believe?
3. Would you want to spend a week at U.S. SPACE CAMP? Why or why not?
4. Why do you think it is important for astronauts to be well trained?

Create and Share   You are at U.S. SPACE CAMP. Pick your favorite day. Write a postcard home describing what happened and what you are looking forward to.

Explore   Look under *astronauts* in an encyclopedia. Find out more information about what type of training astronauts go through.

The
Best
New
Thing

by Isaac Asimov

Part I

Rada lived on a little world, far out in space. Her father, her mother, and her brother Jonathan lived there too. So did other men and women.

Rada was the only little girl on this world, and Jonny was the only little boy. They had lived there all their lives. Rada's parents and other grown-ups worked on the spaceships. They made sure everything was all right before the spaceships went back to Earth or to other planets. Rada and Jonny watched them come and go.

They had to wear their space suits when they watched. There was no air on the little world, but inside their suits there was air and it was warm. Over their head they wore a glass ball that they could see through.

When people came out of the spaceships, they would see Rada and Jonny. They would say, "Think of that! Children live here."

One of the men said, "Would you like to see Earth someday? It's a big world."

Jonny asked, "Are things different on Earth?"

"Well, the sky is blue," said the man.

"I've never seen a blue sky," said Rada. "The sky is always black here."

"On Earth, it's blue, except at night," said the man. "It's warm and there is air everywhere. You don't need a space suit on Earth."

Rada jumped high
to see where her father
was. When she jumped,
she could see all around the spaceship.

She didn't see her father, so she knew he
must be inside the spaceship.

She pushed a button on her suit, letting
some air out. It went s-s-s-s, making her
go down again.

The man said, "You do that very well."

Jonny said, "I can do it too. See?"

He jumped and then made himself come
down headfirst. He landed very softly.

The man laughed and said, "That's well
done, too, but you couldn't do that on Earth."

"Why not?" Rada asked.

"On Earth," said the man, "you can only jump
a little way. Earth is so big, it holds you down.
If you jump up, Earth pulls you down right away.
You could roll down any slanting place."

Then the man had to go into the spaceship
again. Rada and Jonny waited for their father.

When their father came, Rada and Jonny went underground with him. They all lived inside the world, in large, comfortable rooms.

It was warm and nice inside their home. There were books and toys and good things to eat. And there was air for them to breathe, so they could take off their big, clumsy space suits. Of course, even indoors they couldn't run without bouncing high into the air, because the world was too small to pull them down.

Jonny said, "Daddy, is it true that you don't have to wear a space suit on Earth?"

His father said, "Yes, it is. There's air on Earth, just like the air that we have in these rooms."

Jonny asked, "Is the sky really blue there?"

"That's right," his father answered. "There are white things in the sky called clouds. Sometimes drops of water come from the sky. That's rain."

Rada thought about this for a minute, and then she said, "If the ground has water on it, doesn't that make it slippery?"

Her father laughed, and then he said, "The rain doesn't stay on top of the ground. It sinks into the ground and helps make the grass grow. Grass is like a green carpet that grows on the ground. It's soft and very beautiful."

"I'd like to see it," said Rada. "And I would like to feel it too. Will we go to Earth someday, Daddy?"

"Oh, yes, Rada," her father said. "Perhaps we can go soon."

Rada was so happy to hear this that she wanted to put her arms about her father. She walked up the wall to be near his head.

"Thank you, Daddy," she said.

Rada's mother came into the room. She held two containers. She said, "Rada! Jonny! Here's your milk." When she let go of the containers, they stayed in the air.

Jonny moved up into the air and came near the other container. He said, "I don't want to use a straw, Mommy. May I roll the milk into a ball?"

"All right, but be careful not to get any on your clothes," his mother said.

Jonny opened the container and shook it. The milk floated out and made a soft white ball.

He pushed the air with his hands and moved his head next to the ball. He put his lips to it and sucked it in. It was fun to drink milk that way.

His father said, "If you drank milk that way on Earth, it would get all over your clothes. You will have to remember many things like that when you are on Earth."

There were so many new things on Earth to think about. There was air that was everywhere. There were the blue sky and the rain, the wind and the flowers. And there were birds and animals.

The next day their father showed them pictures of some of the new things. They saw that the ground could be flat in some places and hilly in others. Soon they would see and feel all these things for themselves.

But there was one new thing Rada especially wanted to do. She told Jonny about it and he wanted to do it too. They didn't tell their father or mother. It was something they had never done in all their lives. On Earth, they were going to find out what it felt like.

Part II

Rada and Jonny had to make themselves strong for living on Earth.

Their mother said, "Now, Rada, Earth is a large world. It will pull at you hard. You must be strong so that you can walk in spite of all that pull."

Jonny said, "Yes, Rada, you have to be as strong as I am."

But Mother said, "You will have to be stronger than you are now, too, Jonny."

There were springs on the wall in the exercise room. Rada and Jonny had to pull on them. They stood on the wall and pulled on the springs. It took all their strength to move the springs.

Their father was happy. "You are both getting very strong," he said, "You will like it on Earth."

Rada said, "When we get strong, we can go to Earth. We'll see grass and flowers and trees. Most of all, we'll find out about the new thing."

Jonny said, "Don't tell anybody."

One day a spaceship came and their father said, "This is the ship that will take us to Earth."

They all put on their space suits. Rada and Jonny were ready first.

On the spaceship they went to their room. It had chairs with seatbelts.

Their father fastened their seatbelts so they couldn't move. Then their father and mother sat in their own chairs and fastened their own seatbelts. The chairs were very soft.

Then the spaceship started to move. There was a loud noise all through the ship and Rada and Jonny were pushed against the soft, soft chair. They were pushed harder and harder but the seatbelts kept everything all right.

"I'm not frightened," said Jonny. "Are you frightened, Rada?"

"Just a little bit," said Rada. She could see the little world as the ship moved away from it. It was smaller than ever. Soon it was just a dot and then all Rada could see were the stars.

"Can we see Earth, Daddy?" Jonny asked.

"It looks like a star from here. It's that bright one there," said his father.

"Look at Earth, Rada," said Jonny. He was very excited.

Rada looked at the bright star and was happy. Soon she would be on Earth and would know about the new thing. She knew Jonny was thinking about it too.

"Wake up, Rada," said her father. "We are coming down to Earth. Jonny is awake already."

Rada looked out the window. Down below she could see a large, large world. She had never seen anything like it. It was green and brown and lots of other colors too. She could see water, too, and that was blue.

Above all the green and brown and blue and other colors of the Earth was the sky.

Jonny said, "How big everything is!"

They could hardly wait.

When the ship stopped, Rada took off her
belt. She was the first one to get out of the chair.
Jonny was second.

Jonny tried to walk. "The floor is holding my
foot," he said.

"Pull harder," said his father.

Jonny did and at last he succeeded in lifting
his foot from the floor.

"Aren't we going to put on our space suits?"
asked Rada.

"Don't forget, we don't have to put on space
suits on Earth," said her father.

"Oh, yes," said Rada. "That's one of the new
things." She and Jonny were waiting for another
new thing too. They squeezed each other's
hands but they didn't say anything.

They went down inside the ship to get to a
little door that would let them out on the Earth.
It was hard to walk, but they were beginning to
get used to it.

The door opened and they all walked out.
There was flat paving all around the spaceship, as
there had been on the little world. But at the
edge of the paving there was grass. There had
been no grass on the other world.

"My," said Mother, "doesn't the air smell sweet?"

"Oh, yes," said Rada. She could feel the air moving. That was the wind. It blew her dress and her hair.

It was warm and the sun was big and yellow.

Jonny said, "Look how huge the sun is." The sun had looked much smaller from their little world.

"Don't look right at the sun," his father said quickly. "That would hurt your eyes."

Now it was time for the best new thing of all. Now Rada would find out what it was really like.

She said, "Look at the grass. And there's a little hill just like the one in the pictures. Let's try it. Look, Mother. See how I can run."

It was hard to run because Earth pulled at her legs. She ran with all her might to the grassy hill. Jonny was running too.

Jonny said, "I can run faster than you." But they reached the grass together. Both were breathing hard from running.

Then they came to the small hill and climbed to the top. That was even harder than walking, but they made it. They looked at each other and laughed, and then they both lay down on the grass and rolled down the hill. When they reached the bottom, they stood up, laughing and breathing hard.

Their father and mother came to them.

"Are you hurt, children?" their father asked.

"You shouldn't run like that till you are used to Earth's pull," said their mother.

"Oh, but we wanted to," said Rada. "We're so happy because we know, now, about the new thing. It's something we had never done before."

"What new thing?" asked her father.

"We rolled down the hill," said Rada. "We could never do that before, because our own world never pulled us. But it was really fun. I think it's the best new thing of all."

And they ran up to the top of the hill to try it again.

Think About It

1. What was so special about rolling down a hill for Rada and Jonny?
2. List other things that happen on Earth that Rada and Jonny could have named as "The Best New Thing."
3. Could this story ever take place?
4. What would be difficult for you if you were to visit Rada and Jonny's world?
5. How might the U.S. SPACE CAMP help you get ready for a visit to Rada's world?

Create and Share
Pretend you are a reporter interviewing Rada and Jonny on the day they come to Earth. Make a list of five questions you would ask. Work with a partner pretending to be Rada or Jonny. Take turns answering each other's questions.

Explore
Find a book or story that could fit with all the stories in BLAST OFF!

Best Friends

What is the very best ship of all?

Friendship

My Friend Charlie

from the book by James Flora

Why I Like Charlie

My friend Charlie is a pretty good old friend. I couldn't like him any better than I do, even if he owned a pony.

There are lots of reasons why I like Charlie. Here are some:

1. He gives half of whatever he is eating.
2. Sometimes he lets me be the pitcher in the ball game, even though he owns the ball.
3. Charlie never laughs at my nose.
4. Sometimes when I am about to be eaten by dragons, Charlie saves me.
5. Once when I cut my hand, Charlie cried too.

Another good reason is that Charlie can think of lots of good things to do. Let me tell you about some of them.

Charlie Saves a Cat

Cats like to climb up trees, but they sure hate to climb down. Some cats will sit up in a tree all day and cry until someone comes to help them down. Most people don't help cats in trees. They call the fire department. But my friend Charlie always helps cats.

One day Charlie heard a "miaow" up in a tree. That was the day he invented a new way to get cats out of trees.

He went home and got a bucket and a rope
and a fish. He put the fish in the bucket and tied
one end of the rope to the handle. He threw the
other end of the rope over a limb up above the cat
and pulled up the bucket.

The cat smelled the fish and jumped into the
bucket, and Charlie brought the bucket down.

That cat had an elevator ride and a fish dinner
all at the same time. She liked it. Now she won't
leave Charlie, follows him everywhere. Charlie
says she just wants more fish, but I think she
really likes Charlie just as I do.

Charlie Borrows My Dream

"I had a good dream last night," I told Charlie. "I dreamed that I had a two-wheeler bicycle that could go anywhere. I rode it right up one side of a tree and down the other. I rode it up and down all the houses on the way to school. When I got to school, I rode all over the ceiling and sideways across the blackboard. Teacher was surprised."

"Say! That's a real whizzer of a dream," Charlie said. "Let me borrow that dream tonight. Will you? I'll let you dream my rocket-to-the-moon dream. It's a good one, too."

"Sure, Charlie," I said. "You can borrow it tonight."

The next day Charlie said, "I sure do like that old bicycle dream of yours. I'm going to keep it a few more nights and add some nice parts to it."

Charlie dreamed my dream for a whole week
and when he gave it back, it was much better. It
had new parts in it where I ride the bicycle over
mountains and tugboats and under the ocean and
over whales and right into the White House in
Washington. Then the President of the United
States says to me, "You are, without a doubt, the
very best bicycle rider in the whole world," and
he shakes my hand and pins a medal on me.

You can always tell when somebody is your
friend. When he borrows a dream, he always
takes good care of it and fixes it up better than
ever before he gives it back.

Charlie Gets Swallowed by a Goat

Charlie and I were walking on Mrs. Murphy's fence. Mrs. Murphy's goat came up and started to nibble on Charlie's shoes.

"That goat is always trying to eat me," he said. "Today I think I'll let him."

"Don't do that, Charlie," I begged him. "You're my best friend, and I wouldn't want you to get hurt inside a goat."

"Pooh!" he said. "I'm going to let that old goat swallow me, and it won't hurt a bit."

He pulled a photograph of himself out of his pocket. He piled some grass on top of it and gave it to the goat. The goat ate it with one gulp.

"See!" Charlie laughed and laughed. "I told you it wouldn't hurt to be swallowed by that goat."

It was such a goofy joke that I chased Charlie all the way home and rubbed dandelions on his nose.

I wish I could think of good jokes the way Charlie does.

Things NOT to Do

"I'm making a list of things not to do!" Charlie was writing on paper. "It will help me stay out of trouble. Whenever I think of something I want to do, I'll just look and see if it is on this list. If it is, I won't do it."

"I'll help you," I said. "I know lots of things not to do."

Here is the THINGS NOT TO DO list that we made. You can use it if you want. It sure makes life a lot easier for Charlie and me. Maybe it will do the same for you.

- Don't tie knots in snakes.
- Don't step on pigs unless you are barefoot.
- Don't eat the bottoms of ice-cream cones before you eat the tops.
- Don't put worms in your father's shoes.
- Don't put peanut butter on horses or turtles.
- Don't paint your head red.
- Don't dream about monsters.
- Don't give bubble gum to fish.
- Don't sit on crocodiles.

A Picture of All the Things I Am Going to Give to Charlie

Someday when I get really rich, I am going to buy all of these things and put them in a big truck. I'm going to drive that truck right up to Charlie's door and ring the bell, and when he comes out, I'm going to say, "Here, Charlie. These things are for you, because anybody as nice as you should have had them a long time ago."

That should make Charlie happy. Then we can play with them together. I know Charlie will let me.

Best friends always do.

Think About It

1. What one thing about Charlie do you like best?
2. What things would you add to Charlie's "Things NOT to Do" list? Why?
3. Do you think Charlie's friend is a good friend? Why or why not?
4. How does Charlie remind you of one of your friends?

Create and Share Make a list of at least five things that are important for a best friend.

Explore Which book or story has someone in it that you would like for a friend? Share the book with one of your friends.

Gloria
Who Might Be
My Best Friend

from THE STORIES JULIAN TELLS
by Ann Cameron

If you have a girl friend, people find out and
tease you. That's why I didn't want a girl for a
friend—not until this summer, when I met
Gloria.

It happened one afternoon when I was
walking down the street by myself feeling lonely.

A block from our house I saw a moving van in front of a brown house, and men were carrying in chairs and tables and bookcases and boxes full of I don't know what. I watched for a while, and suddenly I heard a voice right behind me.

"Who are you?"

I turned around and there was a girl in a yellow dress. She looked the same age as me. She had curly hair that was braided into two pigtails with red ribbons at the ends.

"I'm Julian," I said. "Who are you?"

"I'm Gloria," she said. "I come from Newport. Do you know where Newport is?"

I wasn't sure, but I didn't tell Gloria. "It's a town on the ocean," I said.

"Right," Gloria said. "Can you turn a cartwheel?"

She turned sideways herself and did two cartwheels on the grass.

I had never tried a cartwheel before, but I tried to copy Gloria. My hands went down in the grass, my feet went up in the air, and—I fell over.

I looked at Gloria to see if she was laughing at me. If she was laughing at me, I was going to go home and forget about her.

But she just looked at me very seriously and said, "It takes practice," and then I liked her.

"Want to come over to my house?" I said.

"All right," Gloria said, "if it is all right with my mother." She ran in the house and asked.

It was all right, so Gloria and I went to my house, and I showed her my room and my games and my rock collection, and then I made strawberry Kool-Aid and we sat at the kitchen table and drank it.

"You have a red mustache on your mouth," Gloria said.

"You have a red mustache on your mouth, too," I said.

Gloria giggled, and we licked off our mustaches with our tongues.

"I wish you'd live here a long time," I told Gloria.

Gloria said, "I wish I would, too."

"I know the best way to make wishes," Gloria said.

"What's that?" I asked.

"First you make a kite. Do you know how to make one?"

"Yes," I said, "I know how." I know how to make good kites because my father taught me. We make them out of two crossed sticks and folded newspaper.

"All right," Gloria said, "that's the first part of making wishes that come true. So let's make a kite."

We went out into the garage and spread out sticks and newspaper and made a kite. I fastened on the kite string and went to the closet and got rags for the tail.

"Do you have some paper and two pencils?" Gloria asked. "Because now we make the wishes."

I didn't know what she was planning, but I went in the house and got pencils and paper.

"All right," Gloria said. "Every wish you want to have come true you write on a long thin piece of paper. You don't tell me your wishes, and I don't tell you mine. If you tell, your wishes don't come true. Also, if you look at the other person's wishes, your wishes don't come true."

Gloria sat down on the garage floor and started writing her wishes. I went to the other side of the garage and wrote my own wishes. I wrote:

1. I wish I'd be a great soccer player.
2. I wish I could ride in an airplane.
3. I wish Gloria would stay here and be my best friend.

I folded my three wishes in my fist and went over to Gloria.

"How many wishes did you make?" Gloria asked.

"Three," I said. "How many did you make?"

"Two," Gloria said.

I wondered what they were.

"Now we put the wishes on the tail of the kite," Gloria said. "Every time we tie one piece of rag on the tail, we fasten a wish in the knot. You can put yours in first."

I fastened mine in, and then Gloria fastened in hers, and we carried the kite into the yard.

"You hold the tail," I told Gloria, "and I'll pull."

We ran through the backyard and into the open field with the kite.

The kite started to rise. The tail jerked heavily like a long white snake. In a minute the kite passed the roof of my house and was climbing toward the sun.

We stood in the open field, looking up at it. I was wishing I would get my wishes.

"I know it's going to work!" Gloria said.

"How do you know?"

"When we take the kite down," Gloria told me, "there shouldn't be one wish in the tail. When the wind takes all your wishes, that's when you know it's going to work."

The kite stayed up for a long time. We both held the string. The kite looked like a tiny black spot in the sun, and my neck got stiff from looking at it.

"Shall we pull it in?" I asked.

"All right," Gloria said.

We drew the string in more and more until, like a tired bird, the kite fell at our feet.

We looked at the tail. All our wishes were gone. Probably they were still flying higher and higher in the wind.

Maybe I would get to be a good soccer player and have a ride in an airplane. And Gloria would be my best friend.

"Gloria," I said, "did you wish we would be friends?"

"You're not supposed to ask!" Gloria said.

"I'm sorry," I answered. But inside I was smiling. I guessed one thing Gloria wished for. I was pretty sure we would be friends.

Think About It

1. What things did Gloria and Julian do and say that showed they were becoming friends?
2. If Julian was to make a list of what he likes about Gloria, like the one Charlie's friend made about Charlie, what do you think he would say?
3. Why do you think Julian would be a good friend to have?
4. What wishes would you put on a wish kite?

Explore   Ask members of your family what they look for in a friend. Make a list.

Create and Share   On a classroom chart or bulletin board, share the list of what your family looks for in a friend.

HARLEQUIN
and The Gift of Many Colors

by Remy Charlip and Burton Supree

Harlequin awoke.

His room was dark and the stars and the moon were still in the sky. It was chilly when he got out of bed, so Harlequin wrapped his blanket around him. And when he walked to the balcony window, he felt as if he were wearing the night.

He saw the shadowy figures of people passing in the street below. They had all left home in the dark to get to the town square early this morning.

But Harlequin sighed, got back into his warm bed, curled up and pulled the covers over his head.

The town square was noisy. It was filled with people busily working. They were bringing great trays of cakes, pies, and cookies, and sawing and hammering wood into little stands where drinks and tasty food would be sold tonight.

The children were all helping, too. They could hardly wait for tonight's great Carnival, where there would be candy and ice cream and dancing and singing and laughing friends and, best of all, everyone wearing a splendid new costume!

295

"But where is Harlequin?" one of the children asked. Harlequin was usually the first one up and the one to lead the others on to all sorts of fun. "I haven't seen him all morning."

"Maybe he was bad and his mother won't let him come out."

"Maybe he's sick. We'd better go see."

And they all ran off to Harlequin's house.

"Harlequin! Harlequin, are you there?" He appeared at the window wearing his blanket.

"Are you all right? Come on out!" His friends all started talking at once.

They were so busy telling Harlequin all the latest news that they didn't notice how quiet and gloomy he was. Slowly Harlequin dressed and came down.

Walking back to the square, the children began to chatter about the new costumes they would wear for the first time tonight. With masks over their faces, no one would recognize them.

But it was hard not to boast and tease with little hints about their costumes.

"Mine is yellow."

"My suit is velvet."

"Wait till you see mine. It's purple."

"What are you going to wear tonight, Harlequin?" They all turned to him.

Harlequin just shrugged his shoulders.

"Oh, Harlequin, you've got to tell. We told you."

"Well," said Harlequin, thinking fast, "I'll wear my blanket as a cape." They thought Harlequin was fooling them as usual.

"Not that old thing!"

"Come on, Harlequin, give us a clue."

"What color is it?"

"What are you going to wear tonight?"

"Nothing," Harlequin replied. "I'm not even coming tonight." And he turned and ran away.

Harlequin not coming? How could that be? How could he miss Carnival?

Perhaps he was teasing. He was always playing tricks. "Wait," one of them said, "I think I know why he's not coming tonight. He doesn't have a new costume."

And it was then that they all realized what was the matter. Harlequin had nothing to wear because his mother was too poor to buy material for a costume. To think of having a good time without Harlequin seemed impossible.

"What can we do?"

"I know! I have an idea. My jacket doesn't need to be so long. I can cut some off and give it to Harlequin. If we each give him a piece of cloth, then he will have enough for a whole costume."

"Yes! My dress doesn't need to be so long either."

"Good! Let's go and get our cloth and meet in front of Harlequin's house."

The sun was directly overhead when all the children met at Harlequin's house. Each one was carrying his gift of cloth.

When Harlequin answered the knock on the door, he was surprised to see all his friends. Then they held out the pieces of cloth and happily pushed them into his hands.

But when the children saw Harlequin's arms filled with the cut-off bits and scraps, they were saddened. Each piece was a different shape and size and color. Some were smooth, some were shiny, and some were fuzzy. None of the pieces matched. They looked like a bunch of rags.

Harlequin thanked them, but the children were afraid they had made matters worse by giving him such a useless gift.

"I feel so stupid," one of them whispered.

Unhappily they said good-bye and left.

When they were gone, Harlequin stared at the scraps of cloth in his arms. "What can I do with these?" he thought. "Nothing. They don't even match, and not one piece is big enough for a pants leg or even a sleeve."

He climbed the stairs to his room, thinking that he would not go out again until Carnival was over.

But as he tossed the heap of cloth onto the floor, one piece stuck to his shirt. He looked at it for a moment. And then he had an idea.

When his mother came home, Harlequin told her all that had happened. Then he told her his idea.

"Do you think if we put all these scraps onto my old suit, it would make a good costume?"

His mother smiled. "I think it would be beautiful," she said.

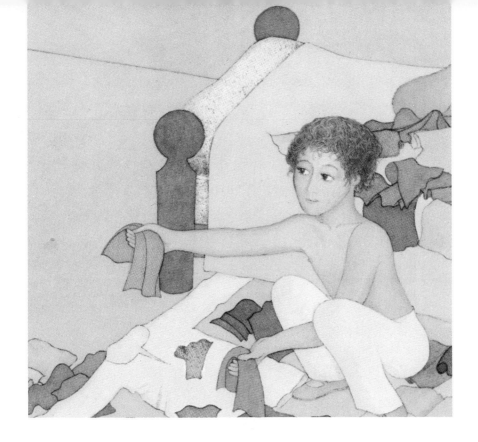

They both set to work. Harlequin chose a blue piece. Then he pinned a green one next to it. He pinned all the pieces where he wanted them, and his mother began to sew them on.

The sewing took a long time, but finally, just before nightfall, his mother finished. She smiled and held up the beautiful rainbow-colored suit.

"It's finished! Let me put it on!"

"How splendid you look," his mother said proudly. He spun around and around, as bright as a butterfly.

"Oh, thank you, I love it," Harlequin said as he put on his mask and his big hat. "It's wonderful!" And in a moment he ran off down to the square.

The town square was wild with color and noise. Harlequin's friends had all come early and were running from one booth to another. But they kept looking out for Harlequin, too, hoping that by some miracle their favorite friend might be able to come.

Suddenly a figure appeared in a costume so splendid that everyone stopped what they were doing. The children all crowded around to see.

"What a fantastic costume!"

"I've never seen anything so beautiful!"

"Who is it?"

"Where is he from?"

"Do you know him?"

No one knew.

Whoever it was, he began to leap and dance and turn so joyfully that the crowd laughed and clapped with delight. All the many different colors he wore gleamed and flashed in the light like jewels.

In a flash one of the children recognized a piece of his own costume. "That piece of blue is mine!" he shouted.

"That shiny red stuff is mine!" said another. "That must be Harlequin!"

"It *is* Harlequin!"

"Harlequin! Harlequin!" the children cheered, as they dashed through the crowd to greet him. They danced around, hugging him and each other with joy.

And Harlequin was the happiest of them all on this happy night, for he was clothed in the love of his friends.

Think About It

1. What problem does Harlequin have?
2. How is his problem solved?
3. Why was Harlequin's costume so special?
4. Tell what you think Charlie or Gloria would have done to help Harlequin get a costume.
5. Who would you like to be friends with the most: Charlie, Charlie's friend, Gloria, Julian, Harlequin, or Harlequin's friends? Why?

Explore   Search in old magazines for pictures of things you would like to give a friend. Cut them out.

Create and Share   Use the magazine pictures you find to make a collage. Share it with your class.

The Gift

by Helen Coutant

Anna left the house at the usual time that morning. It would take her five minutes to run down the hill to where the school bus waited. If she was fast, she could stop by old Nana Marie's house. By now, Nana Marie might be back from the hospital. She had disappeared without warning more than a week ago. Anna could scarcely eat she was so worried. Had they taken Nana Marie to one of those homes for very old people?

Now, going down the road, Anna could see
Rita, Nana Marie's daughter-in-law, standing by
the gate in front of the house. Rita's loud voice
rang out. "She's coming home today! Home
from the hospital! Nana Marie!"

Nana Marie was coming home. Anna's heart
gave a joyful leap.

"We're throwing a little party," Rita went on.
"Just a few neighbors to welcome her back and
cheer her up. Drop by after school. She'll be
looking for you.

"Well, she won't really be looking for you.
But come see her. Nana Marie will need your
company now that she's blind . . . "

Blind? Rita kept talking, but Anna heard nothing more. Her heart seemed to have stopped on the word *blind*. How could Nana Marie suddenly be blind? There had been nothing wrong with Nana Marie's eyes.

Rita started talking again. "Just happened, just like that. It's terrible. But you come by this afternoon for the party. We'll cheer her up. We'll give Nana Marie some little presents to help her forget. Can I count on you?"

Count on her! Had Anna ever missed a chance to visit Nana Marie in the last six months since the two had met and become friends? Every day after they had met she went to keep Nana Marie company. As long as the afternoons were warm they sat on the porch. When cold weather arrived, Anna climbed the steep stairs to Nana Marie's room. Sitting by the window they could see the world just as well as from the porch. They never ran out of things to talk about.

"So you'll come," Rita said.

Anna couldn't answer. She pulled back, nodding, and turned away. Anna took off, filled with anger and sorrow. Her heart was pumping "blind, blind, blind" faster and faster. Blind without any warning. How could it happen? And yet it had.

She got to the foot of the hill just in time to see the school bus disappear. It had gone without her. The tears she had been holding back came to her eyes. There was no way she could get to school. Her mother was already at work. Not wanting to go back to the empty house, Anna headed for her favorite path, which led upward into the woods.

There must be something she could do for Nana Marie. Rita had said something about a present. But what present could ever console a person who had become blind?

Ahead was a place she often came. It was a small deep spring in the woods. When she knelt to gaze into the bottomless pool, at first she saw nothing but darkness. Then as the sun came out, she saw the reflection of things around her. The reflection reminded her of Nana Marie.

Lost in thought, Anna continued to follow the path up the mountain. She decided to stay there until school was out. Maybe by then she would know what to bring Nana Marie.

As the hours passed, Anna picked up objects she thought Nana Marie would like: a striped rock, a tiny fern, a clump of moss, an empty milkweed pod. None of them, on second thought, seemed a proper gift for Nana Marie. There had to be a way to bring the whole woods, the sky, and the fields to her. What else would do? What else would be worthy of their friendship?

Suddenly Anna knew what her gift would be. It would be like no other gift, and a gift no one else could bring. All day long Anna had been seeing the world the way Nana Marie had shown her. Now she would bring everything she had seen to Nana Marie.

She turned and began the long walk back to Nana Marie's house. Her hands were empty in her pockets. But the gift she carried in her head was as big as the world.

Just as the sun went over the mountain, Anna came out from the woods. Ahead of her was the road and Nana Marie's house. She rapped softly on the door. There was no answer. She could see a light in the living room. She knocked again, louder, then put her hand on the doorknob. It opened from the other side, and Rita stood there in her bathrobe.

"Well, here at last," Rita said. "I figured you went home and forgot. The party ended half an hour ago. I told Nana Marie it wasn't any use waiting up for you longer. I expect she's asleep by now. She was real disappointed you didn't come, though she got lots of nice things from everybody. Why don't you come back tomorrow when she's rested."

"Please, I can't," Anna said. "I have a present for Nana Marie. It won't take long. I'll take my shoes off and go upstairs to her room."

Anna headed for the stairs on tiptoe. The landing at the top of the stairs was dark, and the door to Nana Marie's room was closed. Anna paused and let her breath out slowly. What did blind people look like?

Anna's hand hesitated on the doorknob. Then she opened the door and shut it behind her.

Nana Marie's room was pitch black. There was no sound at all. Was the room empty? The window was straight ahead. Anna ran to it. The blinds clattered up, crashing in the darkness. Then a faint light flowed into the room.

"Anna." Nana Marie was calling her name. She was not asleep after all. "Anna," Nana Marie said, and now there was surprise and joy in her voice. Nana Marie was sitting in her rocking chair.

"Oh, Nana Marie!" Anna exclaimed. She patted the old warm skin of Nana Marie's cheek.

"You came," Nana Marie said. "I thought maybe you were getting tired of having such a very old lady for a friend."

"I brought you a present," Anna said. "I'm late because it took me all day to get it."

"Gracious," said Nana Marie. "You shouldn't have done that. All the nice people who came this afternoon brought me presents as if I could see and were still of some use to someone!" She chuckled, pointing toward the table and new stack of boxes.

"Mine is different," Anna said. "I brought you a last day."

"A last day . . . " Nana Marie said. Her fingers stretched out, reaching for Anna. She took Anna's hand and held it firmly.

"You didn't have a last day to look at the world," Anna said. "So I brought it to you. Everything I saw today. Just as if you saw it with me. The way you would see it. And tomorrow I'll bring you another—and the next day another. I'll bring you enough seeing to last forever. That's my present, Nana Marie."

Nana Marie was silent for a minute. Then she added softly, almost to herself, "Bless you, child, how did you ever think of that?" She leaned back in the rocking chair. One hand held on to Anna's. With the other she pointed toward a chair. "Pull it up right here, Anna," she said, "so we can look out over the valley and the moonlight together. The moon is out, isn't it, Anna? I can feel it." She closed her eyes.

Anna pulled Nana Marie's hand into her lap and held it with both of her own as she described everything she had seen that day.

When Anna was finished, Nana Marie sat up and turned toward her. Nana Marie's blue eyes were filled with happiness. "Thank you, Anna," she said. "That was beautiful." She paused briefly and when she continued it was almost as though she was speaking to herself. "*This* is a day I'll always remember."

Anna sat holding on to Nana Marie's hand until the moon disappeared over the house. Even though something as terrible as going blind had happened to Nana Marie, she really hadn't changed. She could still marvel at the world, she could still feel the moonlight. Anna knew she was going to be all right.

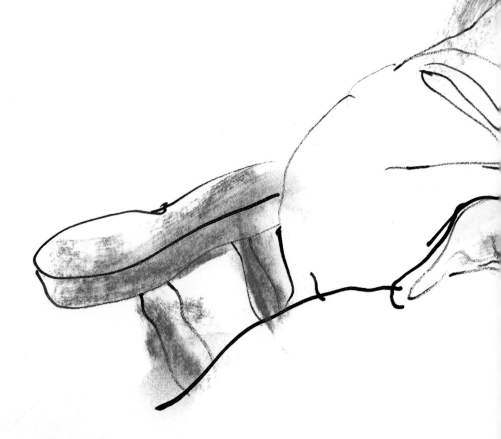

Glossary

Full pronunciation key* The pronunciation of each word is shown just after the word, in this way: **ab·bre·vi·ate** (ə brē′vē āt).

The letters and signs used are pronounced as in the words below.

The mark ′ is placed after a syllable with a primary or heavy accent, as in the example above.

The mark ′ after a syllable shows a secondary or lighter accent as in **ab·bre·vi·a·tion** (ə brē′vē ā′shən).

a	hat, cap	**k**	kind, seek	**ᴛʜ**	then, smooth
ā	age, face	**l**	land, coal	**u**	cup, butter
ä	father, far	**m**	me, am	** u̇**	full, put
b	bad, rob	**n**	no, in	**ü**	rule, move
ch	child, much	**ng**	long, bring		
d	did, red	**o**	hot, rock	**v**	very, save
e	let, best	**ō**	open, go	**w**	will, women
ē	equal, be	**ô**	order, all	**y**	young, yet
ėr	term, learn	**oi**	oil, voice	**z**	zero, breeze
f	fat, if	**ou**	house, out	**zh**	measure, seizure
g	go, bag	**p**	paper, cup	**ə**	represents:
h	he, how	**r**	run, try		*a* in about
i	it, pin	**s**	say, yes		*e* in taken
ī	ice, five	**sh**	she, rush		*i* in pencil
j	jam, enjoy	**t**	tell, it		*o* in lemon
		th	thin, both		*u* in circus

*Pronunciation Key and respellings are from *Scott, Foresman Intermediate Dictionary* by E. L. Thorndike and Clarence L. Barnhart. Copyright © 1983 by Scott, Foresman and Co. Reprinted by permission.

A

ac·cord·ing to (ə kôr′ding tü′) in agreement with; going along with (I decide which coat to wear *according to* how cold it is outside.)

ad See **advertisement.**

ad·mit (ad mit′) to say that something is true, even though you did not want to (When she saw all the money we made, our teacher had to *admit* that the bake sale was a good idea.) **admitted, admitting**

ad·ven·ture (ad ven′chər) an exciting thing to do (Climbing that high mountain was an *adventure* for the group of children.)

ad·ver·tise·ment (ad′vər tīz′mənt) a printed note, often one trying to sell something (We put an *advertisement* in the school paper when we wanted to sell our hamsters.)

al·low·ance (ə lou′əns) a set sum of money (Her mom gives her an *allowance* of one dollar per week.)

ar·ma·dil·lo (är′mə dil′ō) a small animal with a pointed nose and a very hard covering like a shell (When it is frightened, an *armadillo* curls up into a ball.)

ar·range (ə rānj′) to put in order (Please *arrange* the chairs in a circle.) **arranged, arranging**

at·ten·tion (ə ten′shən) the act of watching and listening (You will do better in school if you pay careful *attention* to what your teacher says.)

aud·i·ence (ô′dē əns) people who come together to watch or hear something (The *audience* watched the movie quietly.)

au·thor (ô′thər) someone who writes something, such as a book, story, or play (E. B. White is the *author* of *Charlotte's Web.*)

B

bal·con·y (bal′kə nē) a small porch with a railing that sticks out from an upper floor of a building *pl.* **balconies**

ba·thing suit (bāᴛʜ′ing süt′) something you wear when you go swimming

bo·a con·stric·tor (bō′ə kən strik′tər) a kind of snake that can squeeze things by winding its body around them (The snake wrapped around that branch is a *boa constrictor.*)

bron·to·sau·rus (bron tə sôr′əs) a very big dinosaur that ate plants *pl.* **brontosauruses**

C

cam·er·a (kam′ər ə) something you use for taking pictures

cam·ou·flage (kam′ə fläzh) **1.** a way of looking like something else in order to hide (For *camouflage,* some animals' fur turns as white as snow in the winter.) **2.** to hide by looking like something else (When hunters hide in bushes, they often *camouflage* themselves by wearing green clothes.) **camouflaged, camouflaging**

cer·e·al (sir′ē əl) breakfast food made from grain

char·ac·ter (kar′ik tər) a person or animal in a story

chuck·le (chuk′əl) to laugh softly **chuckled, chuckling**

clue (klü) something that helps you solve a problem or a mystery (The footprints in the snow were a *clue* to who had been in the barn.)

cock·pit (kok′pit′) the place where the person who is flying an airplane sits (The wheel that steers the plane is in the *cockpit.*)

---

a hat / ā age / ä far / e let / ē equal / ėr term / i it / ī ice / o hot / ō open / ô order / oi oil / ou out / u cup /
u̇ put / ü rule / ch child / ng long / sh she / th thin / ᴛʜ then / zh measure / ə a in about, e in taken,
i in pencil, o in lemon, u in circus

code (cōd) secret writing in letters or numbers (During wars, armies use a *code* for their notes.)

col·lapsed (kə lapst′) fallen in (The *collapsed* balloon was flat.)

col·lar (kol′ər) **1.** a band that goes around the neck of a dog or other pet (The name of Carmen's dog is on its *collar.*) **2.** a band on clothing that goes around a person's neck

com·pu·ter (kəm pyü′tər) a machine that is used to do math, solve problems, and work with information

con·struc·tion (kən struk′shən) the act of building something; the way in which something is built or put together (The *construction* of the new school will take a long time.)

con·tain·er (kən ta′nər) a jar, a bottle, or anything that can hold something inside it (Pour the juice out of the *container.*)

con·tents (kon′tents) everything that is inside something (Joe checked the *contents* of his pockets and found a baseball card and two keys.)

con·trap·tion (kən trap′shən) a strange machine or other invention (He made a *contraption* for catching bugs.)

cos·tume (kos′tyüm) clothes worn for fun to make a person look like someone else (Harry dressed up in a rabbit *costume* for the party.)

court (kôrt) the place where people are judged for breaking laws (Because he drove too fast, he had to pay a fine in *court.*)

coy·o·te (kī ō′tē) a wild animal that lives on America's prairies and looks like a small wolf

crick·et (krik′it) a black bug that looks a little like a grasshopper (*Crickets* can jump and chirp.)

cro·quet (krō kā′) a game played outdoors with sticks and wooden balls

D

dan·de·li·on (dan′dl ī ən) a weed with bright yellow flowers (Most people do not like *dandelions* in their lawns.)

de·cide (di sīd′) to make up your mind (*Decide* what you want to do today.) **decided, deciding**

de·light (di līt′) great joy; something that causes joy

de·part·ment (di pärt′mənt) a part of some whole thing, such as a store or a town government (The store has one *department* for books and another one for records.)

des·ert (dez′ərt) a place with hardly any water or trees (All Chris could see for miles was the sand of the *desert*.)

de·sire (di zīr′) **1.** a wish (My *desire* is for my family to be happy and healthy.) **2.** to wish for strongly (The country *desires* peace.) **desired, desiring**

de·vel·op (di vel′əp) **1.** to make pictures come out on film **2.** to grow (The tadpole will *develop* into an adult frog.)

di·al (dī′əl) a disk or circle with numbers or marks around the edge. It usually has a pointer or some other thing that can move. (The *dial* on the washing machine is set so that the laundry will wash for 55 minutes.)

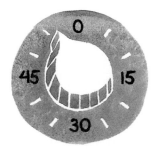

dis·a·gree (dis′ ə grē′) to think differently than; not to agree (Ron and I *disagree*, because he likes baseball and I like football.)

---

a hat / ā age / ä far / e let / ē equal / ėr term / i it / ī ice / o hot / ō open / ô order / oi oil / ou out / u cup / ů put / ü rule / ch child / ng long / sh she / th thin / ᵺ then / zh measure / ə a in about, e in taken, i in pencil, o in lemon, u in circus

dis·ap·pear (dis′ə pir′) **1.** to go away; to stop being (The snow *disappeared* when the weather became warm.) **2.** to go out of sight (The bus went around the curve and *disappeared* from sight.)

dis·ap·point·ed (dis′ ə point′əd) feeling that someone has let you down; made unhappy (Jack was *disappointed* when Rosa broke her promise.)

dis·cour·aged (dis kėr′ijd) feeling as though you should give up; having little hope (When things go wrong, some people get *discouraged*.)

dis·cov·er (dis kuv′ər) to find; to see for the first time (Linda *discovered* a four-leaf clover in the grass.)

dis·guise (dis gīz′) to make yourself look like someone else (Hetty *disguised* herself as an old woman.) **disguised, disguising**

doubt (dout) a problem with believing something; a questioning (I have no *doubt* that you are telling the truth.)

drawer (drôr) a part of a desk or cabinet that is shaped like a box and can slide in and out (I keep sweaters and shirts in the top *drawer*.)

dun·geon (dun′jən) a jail under the ground (The castle had a dark, locked *dungeon*, where the queen put people who stole things.)

E

ea·gle (ē′gəl) a very big bird with strong wings and eyes that can see small things far away (The *eagle* swooped down from the cliff to catch a rabbit.)

earth·ling (ėrth′ling) someone who lives on earth

el·e·va·tor (el′ə vā′tər) a machine that carries people up and down (The *elevator* took Ms. Brown to the 14th floor.)

em·bar·rassed (em bar′əst) feeling uneasy and ashamed (Bob looked *embarrassed* when he made the mistake.)

e·mer·gen·cy (i mėr′jən sē) a time of sudden need or threat (There was an *emergency* when a fire started in the old barn.) *pl.* **emergencies**

e·nor·mous (i nôr′məs) very big (The elephant was *enormous*.)

e·quip·ment (i kwip′mənt) the things you need for something; supplies (Bats, balls, and gloves are *equipment* that you need for playing baseball.)

es·pe·cial·ly (e spesh′ə lē) more than other things; mainly; very (I think daisies are *especially* pretty.)

ex·act·ly (eg zakt′lē) correctly; with no mistake (The answer was *exactly* right.)

ex·claim (ek sklām′) to speak out ("I never thought I would win!" she *exclaimed*.)

ex·er·cise (ek′sər sīz) **1.** the movement of the body to make it stronger (I swim in the pool every day to get *exercise*.) **2.** to strengthen the body by movement (To stay healthy, people need to *exercise* every day.) **exercised, exercising**

ex·pe·di·tion (ek′spə dish′ən) a long trip for a special reason (They went on an *expedition* into the jungle to find a plane that had crashed.)

ex·per·i·ment (ek sper′ə ment) **1.** a test to find out something (I am doing this *experiment* to see whether plants will grow without sunlight.) **2.** to make a test (Mom *experimented* with different kinds of flour to see which made the best bread.)

---

a hat / ā age / ä far / e let / ē equal / ėr term / i it / ī ice / o hot / ō open / ô order / oi oil / ou out / u cup / u̇ put / ü rule / ch child / ng long / sh she / th thin / ŦH then / zh measure / ə a in about, e in taken, i in pencil, o in lemon, u in circus

ex·plain (ek splān′) to tell how or to make clear (Can you *explain* to me how a car works?)

ex·plor·er (ek splôr′ər) someone who goes to new places to learn things about them (I want to be an *explorer* someday and fly to other planets.)

F

far·thest (fär′ᴛʜist) the most far away (Our house is the *farthest* one from school; everyone else lives closer to the school than I do.)

fault (fôlt) a cause for blame (Laura did not throw the ball carefully, so the broken window is her *fault*.)

fer·ret (fer′it) a small animal with white or yellowish fur (In the past, people used *ferrets* to kill rats.)

fetch (fech) to go and get something (When I throw a stick, my dog *fetches* it.)

fig·ure (fig′yər) a shape or form (You can see the *figure* of a man in the lighted window.)

film (film) something used in a camera to make photos (The *film* looked like a little roll of plastic.)

flex·i·ble (flek′sə bəl) able to bend easily (She drank her milk with a *flexible* straw.)

fruit (früt) part of a plant that has seeds and is often good to eat (Bananas and apples are kinds of *fruit*.)

fur·i·ous·ly (fyur′ē əs lē) in a wild, fierce way (The wind was blowing so *furiously* that it bent the trees.)

G

gadg·et (gaj′it) a small tool or machine (This *gadget* is used to crack nuts.)

ga·rage (gə räzh′) the place where a car is kept (There are two cars in the *garage*.)

ge·ra·ni·um (jə rā′nē əm) a kind of plant with pink, red, purple, or white flowers

ghost (gōst) the spirit of a dead person that some people think they can see

glimpse (glimps) **1.** a short look (When the car door opened, we got a *glimpse* of the boy inside.) **2.** to get a short look at (I *glimpsed* a brown cow as our car sped by.) **glimpsed, glimpsing**

group (grüp) a number of people or things together (There was a *group* of chairs in front of the stage.)

gyp·sy (jip′sē) someone who is part of a group of people who probably came from India long ago and now travel from place to place (The *gypsies* camped outside the town.) *pl.* **gypsies**

hawk (hôk) a bird with a hooked beak and strong, curved claws (*Hawks* eat mice and other small animals.)

heav·i·ly (hev′ə lē) in a heavy way (The large bag hung *heavily* on her arm.)

her·o (hir′ō) a person who does good or brave things (The *hero* rescued the child from the burning house.) *pl.* **heroes**

hid·e·ous (hid′ē əs) very ugly (I think that color is *hideous*.)

hol·i·day (hol′ə dā) a day when people do not work or go to school (Thanksgiving and the Fourth of July are *holidays*.)

hor·ri·ble (hôr′ə bəl) terrible; very bad (The smell of burning rubber is *horrible*.)

il·lus·tra·tor (il′ə strā′ tər) someone who draws pictures to go in books or magazines

---

a hat / ā age / ä far / e let / ē equal / ėr term / i it / ī ice / o hot / ō open / ô order / oi oil / ou out / u cup / u̇ put / ü rule / ch child / ng long / sh she / th thin / ᵮн then / zh measure / ə a in about, *e* in taken, *i* in pencil, *o* in lemon, *u* in circus

i·mag·in·a·tion (i maj′ ə nā′shən) the power of thinking up things that are not really there; the power to imagine (He used his *imagination* to make up a story about people from Venus.)

i·mag·in·a·tive (i maj′ə nə tiv) able to make up things; having a good imagination (Marcella always thinks up *imaginative* stories.)

im·pris·on (im priz′ən) to put in jail

in·jure (in′jər) to hurt or harm (Do not *injure* yourself with that sharp knife.) **injured, injuring**

in·ter·est·ed (in′tər ə stid) wanting to know about something or do something (Lee is *interested* in sports.)

in·vent (in vent′) to think up or make something new (Thomas Edison *invented* the light bulb.)

J

jew·el (jü′əl) a shiny, valuable stone; a gem (Her ring had a green *jewel* set in the top.)

jour·ney (jėr′nē) a trip (Carlos made a *journey* to Spain.)

L

leath·er (leṭн′ər) a material made from the skin of an animal (Some shoes are made of *leather.*)

li·brar·y (lī′brer′ ē) a room or building where books are kept (In the *library*, Dorothy found books about model trains and airplanes.)

M

mag·a·zine (mag′ə zēn) a printed booklet that is sold weekly or by the month and that has stories and pictures in it (*Time, Highlights, Ranger Rick,* and *Family Circle* are all *magazines.*)

ma·ter·i·al (mə tir′ē əl) what something is made of (The shirt was made of soft blue *material.*)

mir·a·cle (mir′ə kəl) something wonderful that happens that cannot be explained; a wonder

mus·tache (mus′tash) hair on a man's face above his lip (Dad's *mustache* tickles when he kisses us good night.)

mys·ter·i·ous (mi stir′ē əs) secret; not known; strange (We did not understand Mark's *mysterious* story.)

mys·ter·y (mis′tər ē) something that is not known; something secret (We have not solved the *mystery* of who took the ring.) *pl.* **mysteries**

N

na·tive (nā′tiv) someone born in a place (If you were born in Iowa, you are a *native* of Iowa.)

naugh·ty (nô′tē) bad; not behaving well (The *naughty* child would not go to bed.) **naughtier, naughtiest**

nerv·ous·ly (nėr′vəs lē) in an uneasy or scared way (The small child *nervously* watched the barking dog.)

O

o·bey (ō bā′) to do what someone tells you to

o·pin·ion (ə pin′yən) what someone thinks (It is Lily's *opinion* that fish tastes good.)

op·po·site (op′ə zit) as different as possible (Winter and summer are *opposite* seasons.)

or·bit (ôr′bit) to move around something else (The moon *orbits* the earth.)

or·ches·tra (ôr′kə strə) a group of people playing many different musical instruments (The *orchestra* played beautiful music.)

---

a hat / ā age / ä far / e let / ē equal / ėr term / i it / ī ice / o hot / ō open / ô order / oi oil / ou out / u cup / ů put / ü rule / ch child / ng long / sh she / th thin / ŦH then / zh measure / ə *a* in about, *e* in taken, *i* in pencil, *o* in lemon, *u* in circus

P

pack·age (pak′ij) a box or bundle that has something inside it

par·a·keet (par′ə kēt) a small, bright-colored bird that is kept in a cage as a pet. It has a curved bill and long tail.

pa·tient (pā′shənt) someone who is treated by a doctor, nurse, or dentist (Dr. Davis saw six *patients* this morning.)

pat·tern (pat′ərn) the way in which things are arranged and how they look together (The shadows of the houses made a *pattern* of gray boxes on the white snow.)

pea·cock (pē′kok′) a large bird with beautiful blue and green feathers

perch (pėrch) **1.** to sit on (The cat *perched* on the step.) **2.** a branch or something else that a bird sits on (A sea gull was using our roof as a *perch*.)

pho·to·graph (fō′tə graf) a picture taken with a camera (**photo,** for short)

pon·cho (pon′chō) a piece of clothing used like a coat. It is made from a big piece of cloth with a hole that fits over your head.

pop·u·lar (pop′yə lər) well known or well liked (Most students go to the baseball games, because baseball is a *popular* sport.)

pre·his·tor·ic (prē′hi stôr′ik) having to do with a time long, long ago, before history was written (Some *prehistoric* men and women lived in caves.)

pres·i·dent (prez′ə dənt) the leader of a club, a company, or a country (The *president* of the club makes a lot of decisions.)

prey (prā) an animal hunted by another animal for food (Flies are *prey* for frogs.)

prob·a·bly (prob′ə blē) more likely than not (If you have a cold, you will *probably* sneeze.)

pro·tect (prə tekt′) to keep from harm or hurt

R

ray (rā) a line of light (The *rays* of the sun hit the earth.)

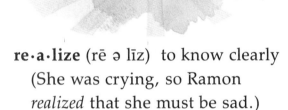

re·a·lize (rē ə līz) to know clearly (She was crying, so Ramon *realized* that she must be sad.) **realized, realizing**

rec·og·nize (rek′əg nīz) to know when seen again (I did not *recognize* Lee in his dark glasses.) **recognized, recognizing**

re·flec·tor (ri flek′tər) anything that turns light rays back (A mirror is a good *reflector.*)

re·lief (ri lēf′) the freeing from worry or pain (It was a *relief* to see that my sister was safe.)

ro·tate (rō′tāt) **1.** to turn about a central point (The earth *rotates* on its axis.) **2.** to move around something else (The earth *rotates* around the sun.) **rotated, rotating**

ru·in (rü′ən) to damage something so badly that it cannot be fixed (The rain *ruined* the newspaper by making it wet and soggy.)

S

safe·ty (sāf′tē) freedom from harm; freedom from danger (Looking before you cross the street is a *safety* rule.)

sci·en·tist (sī′ən tist) someone who carefully watches living things and the world we live in in order to understand how they work (The *scientist* is trying to learn more about the sun.)

seat belt (sēt′ belt′) a strap to hold someone in a seat and protect him or her

---

a hat / ā age / ä far / e let / ē equal / ėr term / i it / ī ice / o hot / ō open / ô order / oi oil / ou out / u cup / u̇ put / ü rule / ch child / ng long / sh she / th thin / ᵺH then / zh measure / ə a in about, e in taken, i in pencil, o in lemon, u in circus

sep·ar·ate (sep′ər it) away from other things; different; apart (We live in two *separate* towns.)

se·quel (sē′kwəl) a story that follows another story. It is about the same things as the first story.

ser·i·ous·ly (sir′ē əs lē) in a way that is not fooling; in a thoughtful way (Mr. Green spoke *seriously* to us about bike safety.)

sev·er·al (sev′ər əl) a few (There were *several* chairs around the table.)

sheep·skin (shēp′skin) the skin of a sheep, often with the wool still on it

sheet (shēt) a large piece of cloth used on a bed (We wash the *sheets* on our beds once a week.)

shep·herd (shep′ərd) someone who takes care of sheep

ship·wrecked (ship′rekt′) of a boat that sinks or is ruined (The *shipwrecked* sailor swam to land.)

shoul·der (shōl′dər) the part of a person's body from which the arm hangs

shut·ter (shut′ər) the part of a camera that opens and closes to take a picture (When I took the picture, I heard the *shutter* click.)

shut·tle (shut′əl) a tool used in weaving that carries thread back and forth across the cloth

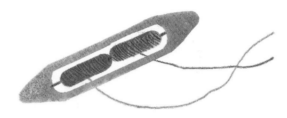

sign (sīn) a note or marker that says or means something (The *sign* for "dollar" is $, and the *sign* for "cents" is ¢.)

slip·per·y (slip′ər ē) sliding and slipping easily (Wet soap is *slippery.*)

slith·er (sliᴛʜ′ər) to slide along (Snakes *slither* across the grass.)

soc·cer (sok′ər) a game in which two teams try to kick a ball between goal posts (There are 11 players on a *soccer* team.)

solve (solv) to figure out or find the answer to (Can you *solve* this word puzzle?) **solved, solving**

space cap·sule (spās′ kap′səl) the part of a spaceship that people and their tools travel in

space·suit (spās′süt) a special kind of clothing worn during space travel that protects a person and lets him or her breathe

spin·dle (spin′dl) a rod or pin that turns around, or on which something turns (The *spindle* in a bicycle pedal lets the pedal turn freely.)

spoke (spōk) a stiff wire that runs from the center of a wheel to its edge. (*Spokes* give support to the wheel.)

strength (strengkth) power; the ability to push and pull (The person who lifted that rock has very great *strength*.)

suc·ceed (sək sēd′) to do well; to do something you are trying to do (After two tries, May *succeeded* in getting the cap off the jar.)

swoop (swüp) to come down in a rush (The owl *swooped* down onto a mouse.)

T

tel·e·vi·sion (tel′ə vizh′ən) a small machine on which you see shows

thor·ough (thėr′ō) complete; covering everything (The vet gave my cat a *thorough* checkup.)

tire valve (tīr′valv′) a part on a bike or car wheel that holds air in

toss (tôs) to throw upward easily (I use a pitchfork to *toss* the hay up into the truck.)

touch (tuch) to be against something (Do not let the baby *touch* the hot stove!)

---

a hat / **ā** age / **ä** far / **e** let / **ē** equal / **ėr** term / **i** it / **ī** ice / **o** hot / **ō** open / **ô** order / **oi** oil / **ou** out / **u** cup / **u̇** put / **ü** rule / **ch** child / **ng** long / **sh** she / **th** thin / **ŦH** then / **zh** measure / **ə** *a* in about, *e* in taken, *i* in pencil, *o* in lemon, *u* in circus

tough (tuf) strong; not easily hurt or broken (A turtle's shell is very *tough*.) **tougher, toughest**

tri·cy·cle (trī′sə kəl) a small bike with three wheels (*Tricycles* do not tip as easily as bikes with two wheels.)

tri·pod (trī′pod) a stand with three legs for holding a camera or telescope

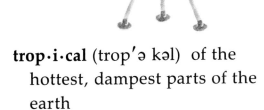

trop·i·cal (trop′ə kəl) of the hottest, dampest parts of the earth

type (tīp) a kind or sort of something (Cats, dogs, and hamsters are all *types* of animals.)

u

un·us·u·al (un yü′zhü əl) not like what you are used to; rare (That juice has an *unusual* flavor.)

use·less (yüs′lis) not having any use; worthless (The broken toy was *useless*.)

u·su·al·ly (yü′zhü ə lē) most often; commonly (In New England, there is *usually* snow in December.)

w

warn·ing (wôr′ning) something that tells about coming trouble (When Mike saw the truck roaring toward the people crossing the street, he shouted a *warning*.)

warp (wôrp) the threads that go the long way in a piece of cloth (The *warp* of the cloth was made of purple threads.)

wea·sel (wē′zəl) an animal about 16 inches long, with short legs, a thin body, and a long tail (*Weasels* are more active at night than during the day.)

wed·ding an·ni·ver·sar·y
(wed′ing an′ ə ver′sər ē)
the day every year that marks
the date when a man and
woman were married (May
first is my mom and dad's
wedding anniversary.)

wil·der·ness (wil′dər nis) a wild
place with no people living
there (The forest was a huge
wilderness.) *pl.* **wildernesses**

wool·en (wul′ən) made from the
fur of sheep (*Woolen* hats are
warm.)

---

a hat / ā age / ä far / e let / ē equal / ėr term / i it / ī ice / o hot / ō open / ô order / oi oil / ou out / u cup /
ù put / ü rule / ch child / ng long / sh she / th thin / ŦH then / zh measure / ə a in about, e in taken,
i in pencil, *o* in lemon, *u* in circus

Thornton, Jane Foster. "**Planet Parade**." Reprinted by permission from *Plays, The Drama Magazine for Young People*. Copyright © 1972 by Plays, Inc. This play is for reading purposes only; for permission to produce, write to Plays, Inc., 120 Boylston Street, Boston, MA 02116.

Whitmore, Elizabeth B. "**Chuka's Hawk**," from *Jack and Jill* magazine, copyright © 1964 by The Curtis Publishing Company. Reprinted by permission of publisher.

Willard, Nancy. **Simple Pictures Are Best**; copyright © 1976 by Nancy Willard; illustrations copyright © 1977 by Tomie de Paola. Adapted by permission of Harcourt Brace Jovanovich, Inc.

Cover/Cluster Openers   Design: Studio Goodwin-Sturges. **Illustration:** Jerry Pinkney. **Calligraphy:** Colleen.

Editorial   Book Editor: Michael P. Gibbons.   Senior Editor: Susan D. Paro.   **Editorial Services:** Marianna Frew Palmer, K. Kirschbaum Harvie.   **Permissions Editor:** Dorothy Burns McLeod.
Design   Series: Leslie Dews.   Book: Bonnie Yousefian, Judy Sue Goodwin-Sturges.
Production   Mary Hunter.

Illustration   **10–11:** Sharleen Collicott. **12–17:** Philippe Dupasquier. **18:** Shel Silverstein, copyright © 1981. from *A Light in the Attic*, with permission. **20–29:** Stephen Kellogg, copyright © 1981, from *The Day Jimmy's Boa Ate the Wash*, with permission. **30–36:** Kathy Spalding. **38–48:** Jan Wills. **52–58:** Ann Strugnell. **61,63:** © The Walt Disney Company. **64,66,67:** © 1981, The Walt Disney Company. **70–84:** Donald Carrick. **88–94:** Marica Sewall. **96–100:** *collage*, Amy Wasserman. **112–116:** Tomie de Paola, copyright © 1976, from *Simple Pictures Are Best*, with permission. **126–132:** Holly Berry. **133–135:** Ron Barrett, copyright © 1970, from *Animals Definitely Should Not Wear Clothing*, with permission. **142–148:** Lulu Delacre. **150–158:** Laliberte. **162–163:** Babette Cole. **164–172:** Fred Lynch. **177–186:** Cat Bowman Smith. **188–192:** Walter Simonson. **196–206:** Susan Spellman. **208–214:** Daniel F. Clifford. **216–222:** Tess Stone. **224–232:** Tony Ross. **236–244:** *title, backgrounds*, Paul Metcalf. **256–270:** Gordon Haas. **274–284:** Eileen Christelow. **286–292:** Ann Strugnell, copyright © 1981, from *The Stories Julian Tells*, with permission. **294–300:** Remy Charlip, copyright © 1973, from *Harlequin and the Gift of Many Colors*, with permission. **306–317:** Glo Coalson. **319–334:** Cyndy Patrick.

Photography   **60–64, 66–68:** *background*, Jim McGrath. **60, 62:** Ralph Mercer © D.C. Heath. **64–65, 68:** © The Walt Disney Company. **136:** Larry B. Jennings (Photo Researchers). **137:** *t*, Stan Way Man (Photo Researchers); *b*, John Gerlach (DRK Photo). **138:** *t*, Robert Maier (Animals Animals); *b*, John Visser (Bruce Coleman Inc.). **139:** *t*, Frank Lane Agency (Bruce Coleman Inc.); *bl*, Zig Leszczynski (Animals Animals); *br*, Photo/Nats. **140:** *t*, John Gerlach (Animals Animals); *c*, Mandal Ranjit (Photo Researchers); *b*, John Eastcott/Yva Momatiuk (DRK Photo). **173:** *t*, Mansell Collection; *b*, Spencer Swanger (Tom Stack & Assoc.). **174:** *tl*, Essex Institute/North Wind Pictures; *cl*, Andy Brilliant; *bl*, Michai Heron; *br*, Joseph DiChello. **175:** *tl*, Michal Heron; *tr*, Bob Daemmrich (Stock Boston); *cl*, Charles Palek (Tom Stack & Assoc.); *cr*, Tim Davis (Photo Researchers); *b*, Peter Chapman; *br*, Photo by Randall and Sally Johnson, courtesy of the International Human Powered Vehicle Association. **234–242:** Ken O'Donoghue © D.C. Heath. **246:** M. Keza (Gamma-Liason). **247:** *t, c*, The Space & Rocket Center, Huntsville, AL; *bl*, M. Keza (Gamma-Liason); *br*, The Space & Rocket Center, Huntsville, AL. **248:** *t*, Guis-Figaro (Gamma-Liason); *b*, M. Keza (Gamma-Liason). **249:** *t, b*, The Space & Rocket Center, Huntsville, AL. **250,** *t, b*, Guis-Figaro (Gamma-Liason). **251:** *t*, M. Keza (Gamma-Liason); *b*, The Space & Rocket Center, Huntsville, AL. **252:** *t*, M. Keza (Gamma-Liason); *b*, The Space & Rocket Center, Huntsville, AL. **253:** *t*, M. Keza (Gamma-Liason); *b*, Guis-Figaro (Gamma-Liason). **254:** *t*, The Space & Rocket Center, Huntsville, AL; **254:** *b*, Guis-Figaro (Gamma-Liason).
Photo Coordinator: Connie Komack.   **Photo Research:** Nina Whitney.   **Photo Styling:** Deborah Bassett, Elizabeth Willis, June Martin.